Life happened before it was over. Then there is the sorting out that empties into overlaid panes, mind's planets, which Bill Lavender navigates in *My ID* with consummate élan and a strong dose of "impolite, unpolitic" dissent.

—Charles Bernstein, author of *Near/Miss*

Bill Lavender's *My ID* traverses a terrain that is at once grounded in the details of an individual life and the collective unconscious, where we cannot always tell if we wake or sleep. Is it an ironic fact that our lives are defined from first to last by Social Security IDs? as the title poem—breath-taking in its condensatory scope—recounts. Koan-like in its dance with the id, as another poem muses: "try to tell the simple truth/ and the repressed slips /out in the accident." Lavender is both erudite and nonchalant, and that's a potent blend. It is a rare pleasure to read poems of such frank and capacious vision, encompassing meditations on mortality (that final exile, "the dream from which I will not awaken"), the aesthetic death of the author ("I can say I but / I can [also] disappear"), and the etymology of Police (the tour de force chapbook which closes the volume). Like the carpenter he once was, with *My ID* Lavender nails it.

—Cynthia Hogue, author of *In June the Labyrinth*

The subject of *My ID* is self-sameness and difference: identity (responsive, shifting, and interdependant) and passage, and to read this book is to ride (as passenger) in a state of balanced satisfaction and *saudade*. "Like Baudelaire," Bill Lavender tells us, "I was homesick / for places I had never been." The beauty of this lucid and loving collection is in the fact that the author is at once at home in the world and also a stranger—an eager, hungry traveler—at home. *My ID* is both poetry and criticism, an extended elegy and a celebration, and a wonderful way to go deep into the world that's changing around us, moment by moment: where, "Even the 'born and raised' are refugees."

—Laura Mullen, author of *Complicated Grief*

In *My ID* Bill Lavender engages and deconstructs the confessional as political act, religious gesture and literary subgenre, all three dovetailing into the Foucault-Derrida-esque essay-poem "La Police." The overall effect is symphonic—each poem gradually builds toward the epic ruminations of "Tui: An Elegy" before leveling off at the philosophical meditations "Of Dreaming" and "Of Sighing." *My ID* is, in the end, a memoir in verse: elegant, wise and enthralling.

—Tyrone Williams, author of *As Iz*

In the name of our precious identity, our supposed to right to privacy, we rankle at the degree to which life is policed. Lavender's poetry explores the antagonisms between the "id" and the ID's which we carry in our wallets. The "id" in its most visceral form emerges, for instance, in tending to the very messy death agonies of a family dog whom one loves with sublime empathy. The "id" and the ID, which is the identity issued by employment, city or state, Olson's polis, are misaligned in so many senses. It is difficult to make a synthesis that can be identified as "my." Lavender probes the liminal spaces between these very different conceptions of what it is to be human, using a supple narrative line, whose pauses and clipped rhythms instruct the reader in how to read and indeed how to feel human. The images and narratives that populate these poems are drawn from a trove of memories or recurring dreams that have obsessed the poet. The materials embody narrative and historical synchronicities, spanning swimming off Grand Isle near New Orleans and camping in Galicia. *My ID* is a serial poem composed of fragments of pilgrimage and rants at the ways in which our nominal lives as citizens have become empty of meaning, despite efforts to find a natural or human balance. Vide the number of times that the poet projects his nude body or intoxicated reveries upon the reader's consciousness. *My ID* is compelling reading and will leave you hungry for more glimpses of Lavender's life and thought.

—Donald Wellman, author of *Essay Poems*

Bill Lavender's ID has never been better defined, though there's some shape-shifting here. Like his other masterwork, Memory Wing, this is a story of identity's quest and chimaera, but this version also invokes the lame quiddity of its artifacts. While the former work winged over the arc of a life, *My ID* swims; the river-course of time includes more of the present, more of the quotidian. Sensitivity to animals, to Spanish pueblos, and to other writers wends its own course that bends the speaker's identity. Where next? we ask one of our finest writers. I'll be along for the ride.

—Peter Thompson, author of *Winter Light*

When one refuses to sell out to metaphysical totality mongering, an appetite for the world as it comes to us—not as it should be—begins to grow. Out of this hunger (not a "yearning" nor "hope"), the perplexity of being a civil among civils, becomes a strength, a ground-clearing series of moments from which a refreshed politic asserts itself. Bill Lavender's *My ID* houses a metric half ton of such cleared-eyed moments. Here are gritty reflections on his life, his city, his region, and globe. Here the purpose of literature is fished out by chance and persistence, not by "method" or "theory." Here notions of human equanimity, is sensibly pursued as work, common work. *My ID* is crack of dawn poetry. What's on your workbench?

—Rodrigo Toscano, author of *Explosion Rocks Springfield*

The world of Bill Lavender's *My ID* is a world of multitudes, of multiplicity, of multiplication. It is a world intensively and intensely described and identified, a world lived, dreamed, imagined, erased, embraced. Critiques of capital, critiques of poetry, critiques of the universal, of the specific. Memories of love, lovers, of deaths, lives, of birth, rebirth. It is so deeply-felt, even at its most casual moments, the reader is not so much invited in as absorbed. "the world is our desire/reflected we are/responsible for what/happens in the world/as we are for what happens/in our dreams." And: "Why must I write? Because not to is to be a tourist." Here is poetry written that demands we enter and breathe.

—Mark Statman, author of *Exile Home*

It is high time to recognize Bill Lavender for the great writer he is, and this book, *My ID*, may very well be the book to do so. Perhaps being known as an extraordinary publisher, festival (co)organizer, construction manager, builder, low residency & study abroad developer, and rock 'n' roll musician has obscured Bill's surpassing excellence as a writer—and stay tuned for the release of his three-novel series. *My ID* manages to blend beautifully Bill's conceptual inventiveness and political-philosophical insights with great, compelling storytelling. Time for us all to sit down, listen, read, & take notice. Damn right!

—Hank Lazer, author of *Slowly Becoming Awake*

In *My ID* Bill Lavender exhibits his Proustian aesthetic of weaving the reader into the poem's nexus via a series of doors opening deep into memory and its nuances. Whether actual identification cards, chickens or Freud's couch, Lavender can take any subject and continue to open it up like a nesting doll, each image varied just enough to cause the reader to adjust to scale. And as you travel along these turns and swerves in the lines, take care: For Lavender's path can suddenly reach swiftly into your heart space churning up the energy of what it means to really peer into life, as seeing and attention are forms of love.

—Megan Burns, author of *Basic Programming*

Everyone has a repertoire of defenses against actually reading a book of poetry. But open Bill Lavender's *My ID* anyway. I guarantee you will be irrevocably glad you did. You might even be delighted, as I was, by various things on every page. Lavender does not play word games, exactly, but rather opens himself up, in a very straightforward way, to the tang and immediacy of ordinary life. He merges with it by means of a clear-eyed testimony, filled with irony and heart. And then the deep humor rises naturally from a Whitman-like care for seeming humdrum details, which turn out to be glowing with mysterious human light.

—Henry Gould, author of *In RI*

Books by Bill Lavender

Three Novellas: Q; Little A; The Private I. Spuyten Duyvil, 2020

surrealismo, (Spanish translation of *surrealism* by Enrique Solinas)
  Yauguru (Montevideo, Uruguay), 2018

La Police, Locofo Chaps, 2017

surrealism, Lavender Ink, 2016

Q, Trembling Pillow, 2013

Memory Wing, Black Widow, 2011

A Field Guide to Trees, Foothills Publishing 2011

Transfixion, Trembling Pillow, 2009

I of the Storm, Trembling Pillow, 2007

While Sleeping, Chax, 2004

look the universe is dreaming, Potes and Poets, 2003

Pentacl, Fell Swoop, 2001

Guest Chain, Lavender Ink, 1999

Bill Lavender

BLAZEVOX[BOOKS]

Buffalo, New York

My ID
by Bill Lavender
Copyright © 2019

Published by BlazeVOX [books]

Printed in the United States of America

Interior design and typesetting by the author
Cover Art (montage of author's original SS card) by the author

First Edition
ISBN: 978-1-60964-352-2

BlazeVOX [books]
131 Euclid Ave
Kenmore, NY 14217
Editor@blazevox.org

publisher of weird little books

BlazeVOX [books]

blazevox.org

21 20 19 18 17 16 15 14 13 12 01 02 03 04 05 06 07 08 09 10

BlazeVOX

Acknowledgments

Poems from this collection have appeared in the following journals and venues. Many thanks to the editors for including them (sometimes in slightly different versions).

Hurricane Review—"My ID" and "Critique of Marx"

Xavier Review—"Foreign Poets"

Southern Review—"T" (from "Tui: An Elegy")

Fell Swoop—"His Genitive"

UNO Poets Anthology—"Writers Retreat (Marginalia)"

Locofo Chaps and LitHub—*La Police*

And thanks besides to the many who, in other ways, helped this book come into being:

Geoffrey Gatza at BlazeVOX, for having faith and making the publication process painless.

Chloe Knopf for careful copy-editing.

Peter Thompson, partner in the struggle, for absolutely everything.

Megan Burns, another partner in the struggle, for helping make New Orleans a safe haven for poetry, even this....

Will and Beth and Roxy and Celeste, the lights of my life.

Ben and Jacqui, the other lights of my life.

Nancy Dixon for giving me the life that made this book and all the others possible.

Contents

Tradition

Knight from the past,
you last
longer than cities
made of words.

Once again, voice
the demands written
on your sleeve, your list
of grunts and slurs.

Show the signs
tattooed on your breast,
rust-stained, hinged
in curious places.

Tell how you
conquered and came
to own this valley
nothing can remember.

Young knight
approaching
from the past,
you're the last.

My ID

1965, I'm 14, at Evelyn Hills Shopping Center
SS office, where my mother brought me to get
my first card, and next door a wallet to put it in,
immigrating to that imaginary nation,
not yet adult but a little closer
to that instilled fantasy of my
self, just so I could wash
dishes after school at the Mountain
Inn Motor Lodge, where I also
took the garbage out and
emptied the rat traps when
they snapped, incredulous when the
little punk my brother's age
in a cheap clip-on tie
fired me, but I got my learner's permit
the same year, wallet in my pocket
on the Honda 50, then diplomas, report
cards, a full blown DL that had to be
renewed each year, first shoplifting bust,
then the checkbook, university ID,
punch card registration,
first friends off to Viet Nam, Leroy
enlisting and reappearing immediately
in a wheelchair, My Lai,
going to class barefoot, first acid trip,
carpenter jobs, car note (my father
co-signed), weekend hops to Little Rock,
first actual sex, third or fourth love,

speeding tickets I threw in the trash,
draft card, first mug shot for a DWI,
first friend with a real camera,
first super 8 art film, first poem
published, first magazine edited, first
degree, first change of address, name
in phone book, first detention at a border
(Canadian), first marriage license, first
photo album that yellowed and split, first
apartment with a lease, first
agreement to buy or sell, first computer
(Apple II-C), title transfer, voter registration,
income reporting dilemmas, learning
to smile for the camera, making funny
faces for friends, guts to take sexy photo
roll to drug store, mortgage application,
act of sale (immovable property),
mastering the art of buying high
and selling low, occupational license, utility
bills, record search at Mortgages
and Conveyances, construction contracts,
bigger-than-pocket-sized checkbook,
car title VI, house title III,
son I, son II, taking them to the SS
office, first book published, university
gig, replacement birth certificate,
life insurance, family plan, IRA started, rifled,
started again, suspicious income fluctuations,
second photo album that yellowed and split,
first fear of audit that never materialized,

bad debt, secret sex, separation of property,
first divorce, Photoshop, ATMs,
first iMac (the beginning of i-everything),
passport, travelers' checks, Mastercard and
VISA, permission to enter, end
of the phone book, second marriage
license, houses VI, VII, VIII, inheritance,
first last will and testament, liquidation of
parents' assets, retiring two hours before
termination of the university gig,
transfer of Roth to regular,
education account for first granddaughter,
education account for second granddaughter,
first smartphone with a decent camera,
veterinary practice taken over by
the old vet's daughter, my sister's cremation
and inurnment, singing tenor to my brother's
melody of when the roll is called up yonder
graveside in the freezing cold, changing
her name on the headstone, transfer of titles
to the remaining plots in the old cemetery,
checking donor on drivers license,
first reading of medicare rules, first
Viagra, even pot getting legalized,
fifty years and that frayed faded
yellowed card with the blue
logo still in the wallet, (on my desk
for inspection as I type), a handsome artifact
in a nostalgic 60s kind of way,
pair of Corinthian columns on either

side, the words "Social Security"
arching over in blue, in red
the sacred number,
eagle in the keystone,
beneath it the caduceus,
snake climbing the torch,
my name typed
on the line below,
and below that the signature
of Bill Lavender.

Critique of Marx

The first station
at the Ralston Purina
Turkey Processing Plant
was the intake platform
where workmen, young guys,
took the live birds
from the truck cages
and hung them by their feet
on a conveyor that took
them immediately through
the electrification tunnel,
which shocked senseless
but did not kill
so the hearts could
continue pumping when
the pneumatic decapitators
snipped off their heads,
retaining the usable necks,
at station 2. After
defeathering at station
3 the birds, still
hanging by their feet,
were slit open and viscera,
excluding giblets, vacuumed
and the carcasses, sometimes
still jerking, blown out with
pressure washers splattering
the workers, still mostly

men at this station
(5), in their white scrubs
and white rubber boots
with water and blood.
(The guts were blown out
the side of the building,
long strings of intestines
hanging from the vent
in the bloody blast,
into a waiting dump
trailer which, when full,
was transferred to the dog
food plant next door.)
At station 6 the feet
were removed and the units
dropped onto a belt. At
the all-female station 7
the giblets and necks
were wrapped in paper
and inserted into the
hollowed-out bodies and
the feet trussed and clipped
in place. Station 8 weighed
and bagged, separating
the traditional holiday
fare into 5 weight categories
indicated by the bag's
color. Station 9, men
again, placed the vacuum-
sealed bags on multi-

tiered racks, each holding
approximately 120 birds,
which were taken by fork-
lifts and pushed into
rooms exactly the size
of the racks. The doors
closed automatically, saving
the forklift drivers,
the most prestigious
workers on the floor,
the bother of stepping
off the machine.
The birds were quick-
frozen at a temperature
of -40 degrees,
then the lift drivers
retracted the racks,
now full of rock-hard turkeys
ready for the grocery store,
and deposited at station 10
(for the lift drivers did
not count as a station)
where they were boxed,
four to a carton,
according to weight categories,
by mixed-gender workers
and sent down a conveyor
to station 11 where I
and four other guys
stacked them on pallets,

again sorted by weight,
5 boxes per row, since
the boxes were designed
with length 1.5 times
their width, 6 rows high
for birds under 12 pounds,
5 rows high over that.
When the pallets were full
the forklifts took them
into the storage freezers
or straight out to the dock
and onto a waiting reefer.
This was
where I worked the summer
before my sophomore year,
the summer after My Lai,
and I had just lost my virginity
to the neighbor girl and was
standing there on the line
swooning from the night before,
and the guy next to me
had a transistor radio playing
"The Battle Hymn of Lt. Calley"
and when I asked him
to change the station
he ignored me, and I
said "Well fuck you then" and he
said "Yeah come on hippy,
fuck me—your asshole'll
be a'singin'."

Imagework

Careful detailing of the shadows formed
in the wrinkled shirt, as if to emphasize his
unfamiliarity with the starched conventions
of the white collar, stirs my memory
of his wanting to like it, wanting to adulate
my sister's skill with the brush (and she did,
after all, intensify the blue of his eyes
and thicken up the hair) but never with-
out derision for the abstract, garish
background attributed to her husband,
the German artist who conquered her
attention in so many ways and certainly
was behind those angry stripes
that so perfectly mimicked my father's
impression of them. Like most paintings
it benefits from a bit of distance, in my case
some six decades, and then the face is good
in an art-class sort of way, glints of light
on the lower lip and forehead
(and from a live sitting), the skin
a bit darker than I remember, as if
captured at dusk, and in the expression
you can see the primal ambivalence
that defined him, mixture of soft-
ness and determination, iron will
and quaking terror. I find my hands
shaking without knowing why
when I look at my sister's masterpiece,

which in brazen disdain he hung
in the basement, over the file cabinets,
where no one ever sat, even as he praised
it, everything but the background, and over
the piano hung a dime-store nature print.
My sister would never again
attempt a work of such ambition.
I view the picture on my monitor, emailed
across the decades from my nephew's phone,
aura of the basement vanished into memory,
into my vocabulary, umber streaks of anger,
yellow ochre of desire, Terre Verte
of despair, Tyrian Purple, Jupiter surface,
the face merely a cross-stroke of similar
tones, and I realize what he hated
was what he said he loved,
not the ground but the figure,
thin visage of himself barely
distinguishable from the cascade
of forces behind him, field
broken only by the wrinkled white
shirt out of which the head,
tortoise-like, emerges.

Structures

All my life I have dreamed of buildings
without knowing it, thinking the matter
of my dreams was in the furtive wandering
through them, the structure mere backdrop,
simple container for the ostensible drama
that unfolded within, not realizing that the
confused searching, anxious frottage and
sudden revelations all stemmed from the building's
psychic funneling. My earliest dreams
were of an utter abyss, terrifying in their
emptiness, prompting me to use the carpentry
I was taught from a young age to erect
these ramshackle protections, with their
tilting walls and flimsy railings, out of salvaged
lumber, scraps gathered from the railside,
ancient splintered studs and broken beams
which split and twist as I toenail them together
into rickety stairs and sloping balconies, passages
connecting one house to the next, ladders
leaning roof to roof, with cantilever beams
rotten as paper, sidings unpainted, weathered
and cupped, shattered clerestories lighting
stairwells webbed with dust, hallways that narrow
to a suffocating point then open onto rooms
crowded with family or workers or travelers
or party guests through which I search
for a half-forgotten lost thing—was it my guitar
that I left in the first room? or a notebook

of important writings? Despite the crowd I
am alone in the house, isolated by forgetfulness,
ashamed that I can't recall my reason
for being there and so pretending to a purpose.
Is this building a school? An airport? Exhausted,
we huddle on the floor and wait for the next
event, and it is within the waiting that the plot
unfolds, the lust and confusion and miraculous
transformations that become the stories
I tell over breakfast, forgetting the six walls,
the mantels and hearths, the newels in the middle
of the room. A black horse is coming down
the stairs, panic in its eyes, but the jewels
in the railing look on calmly and the dumbwaiter
ascends with aplomb. The triangular garret
opens onto the widow's perch and from there
I can get onto the roof, slippery with vertigo
until I catch myself on a protrusion, not daring
to look down into the dark courtyard littered
with broken masonry and glass. Sometimes I have
to go to work, hunt down my tools to jimmy
a lock or open a wall to resolve a cul-de-sac.
The dust of old dead plaster falls in my hair
and in my eyes, grit of an imagined past between
my teeth, or I take refuge in the damp cellar,
shadows shifting in the corners, jars on the
shelves, my head bumping the exposed joists
of the ceiling. The room where I left my newfound
friend is not there when I return from searching
for my laptop which I remember leaving on the kitchen

counter, in its place a library, scholars engrossed
in ancient texts, handling their folios with white
gloves, but then I spot her behind the credenza,
reclined as at a picnic yet brooding and uninterested
in my discovery. The drawers hold oddments,
bits of cloth and fur and dissembled electronics,
cricket cages, binoculars, jeweler's pliers and—
the motion catches my eye—a cicada struggling
out of its molt. The back yard, shaded by a canopy
of rusting tin, has been picked bare by mud-stained
chickens roosting in the braces; I glimpse them
briefly through the window as I pass, rubbing
my hand along the wainscotting, feeling a flush
of disappointment in the roughness of the finish
but called urgently on to rescue the forgotten one.
The houses of my dreams are connected by tunnels
and catwalks across daylight hours, a single great
edifice bristling with wind vanes and steeples and
crenellated battlements, minarets and turrets,
stone archways and crumbling towers, hotel
for my hordes, impregnable fortress.

First Subjects

They were dressed in formal wear, propped
and sewn into chairs, their visages burned
onto plates of silver-plated copper or glass.
These complacent customers were the first
commercially viable tenants of the new techne,
daguerreotype, and budding entrepeneurs
rushed to meet the demand.

Carefully groomed and dressed in the latest fashion,
they were ideal subjects for the early experiments,
holding their poses faithfully and not troubling the
artist, engrossed in the tempermental mechanisms,
by fidgeting.

They are the outliers of History, these dead,
ghosted darkly onto glass, captured
at their precise moment of disappearance,
engraved onto eternity in a way
no one before them could boast.

Before the chemistry advanced to allow
for manageable exposure times, vital subjects too
were tied to posts and chairs, t-shaped rods
run up the spine and along the shoulders, beneath
jackets and evening gowns, crucifying the bourgeois
with interminable sittings, even breathing prohibited.

Freud's Office

Photograph of a cave drawing
on the wall, and a litho
of the Charcot painting[1], African
masks, darkly weathered grain
of the panelling and desk,
tufted leather, smell of brandy
and cigar smoke, prayer rug
on the storied couch, Anna's
imprint still fresh from the trance,
though the work began with
language, with aphasia, not
with images per se. What is
the difference between desire
for incest and its enactment?
having lusted in the heart
which absence of course
makes fonder… though
the absence, one ultimately
learns, is of the subject itself,
the heart in third person
neuter, I and it and super-
I coupling in coetaneous
cradles when the stand-in

---

1   André Brouillet's 1887 A Clinical Lesson at the Salpêtrière depicts
     Charcot demonstrating hypnosis to his medical students, a crowd of
     thirty black-suited men. The subject, a young woman in rumpled
     white blouse slipping down from shoulder and bodice, has swooned
     into the arms of an assistant. Freud had a lithograph of this painting
     placed over the couch in his consulting room.

oozes out like a droplet,
unspoken, dreaming
of punishments, eyeing you
and him and her, jealousy
and other delicious nectars
dripping from her pronouns,
pleated linen of the perambulator
passed down from the neolithic
or at least the Greek,
memorials traced in wet folds,
or was it actually Vienna,
just Vienna caught up
in the academic hustle,
on the couch?
At any rate, the "discovery"
went unnoticed up the road
at Braunau am Inn[2], so
the tyrant's conception
and/or birth stayed on schedule,
the books were ceremoniously
burned and things left to run
their bloody, phenomenal course
all over bloody Europe,
and in every bombed-out city:
a camera on a tripod.

---

2   Birthplace of Adolf Hitler.

Scrawl

Of all the myriad pro-
ducts of late
capitalism, of all
the plastic gee-
gaws made in China
and shipped to the
states by the grosses
of grosses to
decorate the walls
of gift shops
and drug stores
and big box emporia
in colors tasteful
or loud, of all
the electronic gad-
gets and applets,
wide-screened and narrow,
smart phones and dumb,
cranked out of
factories in exo-
tic lands, crafted
by robots or young
women or their children
chained to the line
16 hours at a time,
of all those com-
modities that give
the convenience of

disposability, lighters
and pens, gloves and shoes,
flatware and stem,
software and hard,
of all those vacu-
formed polymer ex-
trusions stamped out
to house their sister
products, blister
upon blister
with well-planned holes
for insertion on
pegboard or slotwall
and a good flat
surface for the bar
code not to mention
theft prevention,
of all those signs,
symbols, artifacts
and solutions
circulating through
the great myst-
ical body of the
world, making
their fran-
tic way from fac-
tory to landfill
barely touching
en route any-
thing that one might

in fairness
to the language
call an end
user, in all this
sea of worthless and
poisonous debris grad-
ually filling the
giant dead cess-
pool of the ocean,
surely the most
worthless,
the least memorable,
the least significant
and most erasable
cipher in the imag-
inary text we call his-
tory is the con-
sciousness of the
common American mid-
level bureaucrat,
who from office and
cubicle, windowless and
close or spacious
with a fan-
tastic view, too
cold or too hot or
just right, decorated
with the faces of
children or grand,
girlfriend or boy,

with posters and post-its
and reminders and forget-
me-nots, dilbert cartoons,
aphorisms and clippings
and stickers cluttering
every surface, or
as minimal and pris-
tine as an Apple
commercial, from their
offices in universities
or corporations or
governments or prisons
or hospitals or schools,
on wall street
or small streets,
on their pneu-
matically cushioned
chairs with ergo-
nomic back support
or their weird
kneelers from which
they appear to be
praying to their
computers or their
yoga balls or ham-
mocks or crappy
stackable units
that came with the
cubicles or cheap
folding metal, where they

answer their phones with-
out taking their eyes
off their screens,
screens with 28 open
windows and 14
programs running in the
background, spreadsheets
and word processors
and databases,
chat rooms and youtube,
productivity enhancers and
time killers, talking
on the phone and
chatting and text-
ing at once, for-
getting where they
were, typing what
they meant to
say and saying what
they meant to type,
meaning exactly
what they meant
not to mean, and
within this nexus,
from within the cy-
cle, falling in love
with the guy down
the hall or in the
next cubicle
or with the boss

or with the dark-
skinned secretary or
the red-haired boy-
genius, or just
aimlessly yearning
with that churning
in the pit of the
stomach, longing for
companionship or
anonymous sex,
for a mate,
for a date,
for a good time
in toilet stall,
sneaking a peak
at match dot
or snatch dot, day-
dreaming of
sucking or fucking
or kissing or pissing
or of sweet re-
unions with childhood
friends, relationships
of deep and
lasting affection or
flash of a face
at the moment of
parting, images that
live in the deep
heart's core sil-

ently, never
spoken of, sud-
denly welling up
in mind's eye,
moments
of thun-
dering emotion,
of great grief
or chilling terror,
when the shadow
of death passes over,
moments gotten past
by returning attention
to the spread-
sheet, the form-
ula, the critical
path, the e-
mail or the text,
the bill of lading
or the game of sol-
itaire, sometimes
even from home,
working from home
since the job can be
done from anywhere,
any place with
a connection,
processing sales,
combing data-
bases in their pajamas,

saving commuting
costs and passing that
savings along to the
consumer.

Grand Isle

All along Caminada Pass now the rip-rap
is unbroken, stone wall between the unrelenting
waves of the western Gulf and the delicate
southwest point of the island. The chenière
that rooted the ground on this end was swept
away by Katrina, leaving a small acre of sea
oats now being trampled by backhoes
and dump trucks. They have covered the beach
with rubber for a good way there
and laid out great canvas socks of sand
to reinforce the bank. Time will
tell how these hi-tech measures work,
but the lee corner between the end
of the jetty and the beginning
of the beach still seems to attract
bottom-feeders, redfish and drum and
of course hardheads, and we meet a guy
who says that the day before he caught
more than a hundred specks right up
on the beach, in two feet of water, pulled
one in on every cast. If he'd been
keeping them he would have limited out
three or four times at least.

Ben and I catch nothing but a couple
of hardheads and six undersized redfish
so we head back to join the others
who have decided to take in the 89th

Annual Grand Isle Tarpon Rodeo at the pavilion
down on the East end by the Coast Guard
Station and State Park, but we are too late
to catch the festivities and meet them on the road.

We pull into the new "Wakeland"
and watch the teenaged boys scoot back
and forth on the waterboard, pulled by
a cable controlled by another teenaged boy
with a joystick. Roxy wants to do it
and we have to explain she is too young
and needs to know how to swim better
before she can try anything like that.
She keeps climbing down the pier-wall
and making the adults nervous. She knocks
my Bud-light into the water and has
to retrieve the can, so I hold her by her feet
and lower her down. She screams at
first about her dress hanging down over
her head, the first time I have heard
her worry about such a thing, and I know
she is awakening to the adult world.
The adults are a little loopy from rodeo
daiquiris and now that we are confirmed
fishless the question of supper arises, so
we rearrange seating in the two cars and Beth
and Roxy ride with me and Ben down to
the Sure-Way to buy some fish to grill.

The Rodeo is winding down for the day

and the frat boys in their muscle trucks are
promenading down Highway 1, subwoofers
thudding and bikini'd party girls dancing
in back, and we slow to a crawl as we
pass party after party with rap music
or heavy metal blaring.

                       When we finally
make it to the Sure-Way they have no fish
and we remark the great irony that we
have just come from the weigh station
at the Rodeo where we've seen a nine foot
marlin, a grouper that could have swallowed
Roxy whole, some fifty pound reds and dozens
of other huge fish all laid out on ice yet
we can't find a piece of fish to buy
on the entire island, the closest thing
being frozen fishsticks which look
suspiciously like McDonalds, which, I hear,
buys all the marlin anyway.

Suppose you had a friend and not just any
friend but a friend of many years, a friend
you might have called your best, a friend
most especially within the art, within
the society of poetry, and one day
as if by metamorphosis this friend
ceases to be a friend and becomes
what you could only call an enemy,
disseminating lies and rumors

and actively campaigning against you.

How long before this island, the big island,
dissolves back into the sea like the
Chenière Caminada? Islands, like people,
are of finite duration, especially these
alluvial mounds of pure sand, accretions
of humus and glass dropped by the river,
built up by the waves and finally pulled down
by those same waves. One would need to be
as mobile as a bird to nest on one, as I suppose
we are, these extravagant camps periodically
reduced to piles of sticks by storms
while their owners worry back in New Orleans
or Baton Rouge or Lafayette, and old
bare pilings stand around Caminada Bay
like remnants of Spanish language in the argot.
Playground for the rich ever since they
cut the canal and boat service opened,
home of second homes for French
Quarter traders, where wives and children
might summer, and then the big shot
of oil money mid-20th century that brought
the entire matrix of rigs and refineries
and canals, dredging the passes to keep
the equipment moving, filling the east
end of the island with the Apache GITB
GOM Shelf facility parking lot,
an acre of pickups baking in the sun,
right next door to the State Park Lagoon

where we kayak after the kids leave.

The stagnant tepid lake is aboil
with ostensible redfish, but whatever
they actually are, they do not bite
anything we throw out. Their implied
though always denied promise keeps us there
past the time we should be out
of the sun and our legs, unaccustomed
to being laid out horizontal in a broiler, blister.

Insatiate the next morning I go down
into the surf early, wade the 50 yards
out to the sandbar and stand knee deep
throwing a gold spoon. The day is
slightly overcast and the sunrise stunning.
Porpoises breach in the light chop and
mullet swarm on the surface. An hour
yields me two keeper specks, enough
for supper at least, and I wade in absently
with my stringer. The surf is frothing
just at shoreline, and I see within it
a five foot tiger shark, the dorsal and tail
and even the bare back well visible over the
six-inch-deep foam and close enough I could
easily tap him with my pole. I freeze and
watch him calmly pass, first shark
I have seen on the beach, and then from
the safety of the sand watch him make
his round, westward down the beach,

always hiding in the froth, then out into
the channel and back east, dorsal breaking
surface now and then making
a dotted line of his progress.

By Monday evening every trace of the rodeo
is gone and the camps on either side of us
are empty. Beer consumption (mine) begins
at 10 (a.m.) and at 2 I fall into a three hour
nap. Sunset. Walking the dog on the beach.
Falling asleep during the movie on AMC.

At 3:30 I wake up and feel my way through
the darkened house to pee, then go
to the kitchen for a bottle of water
and drink it down. Then I go back to
bed and lay there thinking about my
friend, or former friend, as it seems
quite irremediable now. I remember
teaching one summer in Madrid,
we were talking about dreams and
one of the students, Summer was her
name, told a dream in which
an "ex-friend" comes to see her, and my
comment was "What is an ex-friend?"

We go out in the evening, Nanc having
scoffed at my fear of the shark, and from
the sandbar hook a couple which get away.
One is a Spanish Mackerel which jumps

insanely when hooked, leaping six feet
out of the water, flipping himself off the hook
before I can get a net under him. We plot
an early morning return to the lagoon with
the kayaks. I'm mad at her because she came
out without her shirt and no amount of sun-
screen will protect you completely. It's six
o'clock she says, and I ask what difference
that makes since the sun is still high in the
sky. We hear a splash and look to our right
just in time to see the shark thrashing with
something on the surface 50 feet from us.
"I'm going in," I say, and she follows.

We pack the kayaks on the truck that
evening so we can just get up and
go and eat breakfast later. No need to set
an alarm of course; I wake up at 5 and we are
launching the kayaks by 6. The redfish
still cut the water all around and still
refuse to bite anything we show them.
I row around trolling with my spoon,
try bait living and dead, a sparkle beetle:
nothing. Finally, all the way at the end
where a short rock jetty separates the lagoon
from Barataria Pass, something bites my
spoon and I land it. It is not a fish I have
ever seen before. Perch-shaped but meatier,
small-mouthed, it looks suspiciously like a
bass except for an overall reddish tint.

The eyes are wild, yellowish red around
the pupils. I keep it, even though I don't
know what it is, and then catch two more.
I get out and walk the rocks, like the proverb-
ial cow, fishing the gulf side. I get
hung in the rocks and lose one rig, two.
I land one speck and then, to my great
surprise, on a spoon, a nice little flounder.

Foreign Poets

Eat local, shop local, read local,
travel local; it seems noble and right
("Breathes there a man with soul so dead…" etc.)
at least when you don't think
about it too hard. When there are
as many Starbucks in Madrid as in
Seattle and as many McDonalds in Paris
as in L.A., cities compete
for the most Disneyfied re-
invention of their vanished pasts,
for the most colorful culture,
for the highest quotient of
smiling, well-dressed people
frozen in front of old buildings
on perfect blue sky days,
vacationing in a localness denied
them in their own localities.

I never warmed to the concept.
Like Baudelaire, I was homesick
for places I had never been.
I craved different weather, different food,
different places, different language—
Poetry was promise of this difference,
poetry not in the sense of what
was fed to us at school, but the impolite
unpolitic stuff we found after, more
to do with bathroom walls than English class.

We farted during the pledge of allegiance
and that was what the poems grew out of.

I loved everything unamerican, nonsensible,
chaotic, incantatory. I liked language that
had to be translated, books with hieroglyphs
on one face and a stammering, inconclusive
English on the opposite. En face even fucked
with the sacred mechanism of the book, setting
up a homosocial page order where rectos
follow rectos and versos versos rather
than the standard hetero verso recto.

Did it all spring from those poetic arguments,
Spicer et al, mostly just Spicer,
who listened for aliens from the local dive
& lived an exile's life within his itty bitty
San Francisco scene, a lot like Maddox
did in New Orleans, and they both drank
themselves to death, for what is
a city but a gathering of exiles,
water-hole for refugees, devoted
locals come to escape their former locales
where the small-minded provincialisms of small
towns prevail, where everyone knows everyone
and they all frown on cynicism, extreme
literacy and alcoholism, and no one even
knows what linguistics is and really no one
has read *Finnegans Wake*?

Even the "born and raised" are refugees.
The city changes under the feet
of those who plant themselves in it,
pristine neighborhoods turn ineluctably
into grubby blocks of sagging shutters,
and the austere ruins of urban slums
get new coats of paint and swimming pools
and are gradually taken over
by white-collar migrants from another state
with bumper-stickers that admonish us
yet again to embrace the sainted local.

The signified, says Todorov, denotes
a lack, a kind of nostalgia for the thing
that announces itself only
at its moment of disappearance.
Our sudden love for the local
is occasion to mourn its passing.

And for the true refugees, those
who leave their homes under
plumes of smoke as they
are erased by the advancing
armies of modernity, two sides
wanting nothing from a locality
but its strategic location, to be
a local—to belong somewhere,
to live where people know
and respect you and assist
when natural or human

brutality threatens to starve
or to evict you— must seem
an impossible dream,
always and only, henceforth,
for foreigners.

His Genitive[3]

the last time i was in paris
i met up with joe who
happy to be speaking
english again told me
of his efforts at foreskin
restoration he was
doing orgasm work
(alone) coaxing the flap
back into existence
with a cock ring
this to increase
his genital
sensitivity the glans
calloused from all
those decades chafing
against his jeans
and to disguise
the wrinkled mark

---

3   The "his-genitive" was a linguistic curiosity of Early Modern English, a great misunderstanding evolved, apparently, from the audible similarity of the genitive -es ending of Middle English and the masculine possessive modifier ("his", as if possession could not be imagined except in the masculine gender). Often described, now, as "folk etymology," this *méconnaissance* was in fact canonized in literature of the era, e.g. John Lyly's *Euphues His England* (1580), the poem *Willobie His Avisa* (1594), the travel accounts called *Purchas His Pilgrimes* (1602), Ben Jonson's *Sejanus His Fall* (1603) or John Donne's *Ignatius His Conclave* (1611), a satire of Jesuit evangelism. The apostrophe we use today was subsequently adopted, mimicking the fashionable French, to indicate the elision of the imaginary hi-.

of elision he bore
such nostalgia for
a vanished bit of skin
stolen from him not in
brit milah nor even by his
jesuit teachers at loyola
but an obsolete
medical fashion
rabbi saadia gaon says
a thing is complete if
it lacks nothing but also
possesses nothing unneeded
thus by amputation
is man completed
perhaps that's the logic
by which the pleonastic
his was removed
from his that is the
king his english
leaving only apostrophe
just that little un-
needed dot floating
ghost-like above
the text to mark
the place of absence
and who could have
guessed uncut would
come around again
such long and anxious
strife to return to joe

living in the suburbs
outside paris almost
30 years now
and completely fluent
his foreskin

Tui: An Elegy

T

(aka Renny, July 14, 2002–June 29, 2018)

we took turns carrying the grief
as if we were lugging a great weight
across a bridge and spelling each other
with her arguing now through her tears
that we should go ahead and put him down
and then saying god look at him he's doing great
today and i'm not going to put him down
just for our own convenience just because
we're taking a trip and me at times
playing the part of the tough country
boy and thinking like my mother who
loved animals sure enough but had dressed
enough chickens and rabbits to have
no qualms about sending one off if
that was the expedient thing to do
for the sake of either the animal's or
the master's comfort and just shaking
my head like my mother used to and
saying i think it's time and then taking
him for a walk and coming back and saying
to nanc i'm not going to be able to put him
on the table if he walks into the vet all
springy with his ears pricked up like he
just walked with me and so talking to

beth she said they would keep him while
we were gone and we knew they would
but we felt bad because he really is
a lot of trouble right now he paces all
night has to be let out at least four or five
times a day and even then has to sleep
on pads because he wets the bed and
even occasionally drops a turd on the floor
and that incessant anxious pacing like
he's always looking for something or
always wanting out but if you try to let
him out or give him what he wants he doesn't
really want anything turns up his nose
even at his favorite treat and then he
barks at the door like he wants to walk
but if you take him out he falls down
the steps and then after about half a
block he starts to pant and hang his head
like some mule who just plowed a hundred
acres and you wonder if he can even
make it back to the house and so we just
felt like it would be too much of a burden
for will and beth since they are busy
and have their own dogs plus of course
the girls so we interviewed this special
needs pet sitter who seemed ok she
charged forty-five dollars per night and it would be
twenty nights kind of a lot but we were ok
with the money if he was going to be well
cared for but then it occurred to us that

we'd rather see that money go to will and beth
than a stranger so we talked to them about
it and it felt more right to leave him with
someone who loved him almost as much
as we did and the money sort of bought
indulgence for our conscience so that was
the way we were thinking to go and this
was only about ten days out from nanc's
heading to portugal but then that afternoon
i walked him down to triangle park and i was
sitting on the bench talking to my analyst
through the earbuds and T comes and
stands right in front of me arches his back
and poos and his back legs are shaking
with the strain like they sometimes do but
this time they give out under him and
he falls back into his own mess and he
starts trying to pull himself out of it
pulling with his front legs and dragging
his butt in the grass which fortunately
cleaned him up a little bit and i helped
him up and got him home but when i told
nanc about it she started crying and said
but that's that's where we always said
we would draw the line when he fell in his
own poo that's when we're going to do it
and i said well maybe we can leave him
with will and beth and just set it up with
nicole so that they can take him when the time
is right and she cried even harder saying

no we're not putting that on them it's not
fair and besides i have to say good-bye
i can't leave him knowing he won't be
here when we get back and i say but now
we're back to doing it to fit our schedule
and she wails the more saying she should
have canceled we shouldn't be going now
but that's what we said when he fell in his own
poo that was going to be the dividing line
and i said ok i'll call nicole monday morning
and i did but she couldn't come to the phone
and she had this new assistant who didn't
know how to spell renny and that made me
mad and i spelled it out very slow and loud
like she was an idiot and then felt bad about
it and nicole called back a few minutes later
and i say nicole we've decided and that was
all i could get out and just stopped and couldn't
breathe couldn't make the words and nicole
is waiting patiently because she knows what
i'm going to say and when i finally blubber it
out we make the appointment for friday which
is only two days before nanc is leaving but
we want him to have as long as possible
even if it means she gets on the plane still
crying and so we text beth and will and
they want to come over sometime during
the week and say goodbye and we set
that up and that evening i'm walking him and
ann marie who lives around the corner

is on her porch and says how's he doing
and i tell her and she says have you tried
cbd oil and i say no where do you get
it and she goes inside and comes back
with a little dropper bottle and says give
him a drop or two see what happens so
i try that and the next time i walk him he
is doing great and i talk to nanc about it again
and she just says oh god should we call
it off and i say let's wait and see we've still
got time and that night we go to bed and sleep
for a couple of hours and then renny
gets up and starts walking around the house
i can hear his claws clicking on the wood
floor as he tracks from the bedroom up
front to the living room back to the kitchen
and then starts the round again and i can
see him in the dim light head down panting
like he's exhausted looking for a place
to rest and i get up and let him out and
he wanders around our little city yard
while i stand naked under the moon
and then he comes back to the door
and i let him in and he starts his rounds
all over and i lie in the bed and listen to him
walking and panting and it occurs to me
that he's looking for a way out like all
the way out out of the house out of the yard
out of the city out of the world primal instinct
of the old and weak to leave home to die

not to slow down and endanger the pack
but stuck here in the human world the only
escape is death itself so he's looking for his
death around every corner in the dark
and he paces all night while we listen from
the bed and finally he lies down just when i have
to get up and go to work and that evening once
again he is doing great on his walk and again
we talk about calling nicole to cancel but we
go to pals for a drink with jessica and jim and come
back in about an hour to find a trail of diarrhea from
the front door to the back and the house stinking
and him trotting around in a panic to get out
so we let him out and he goes around and
around the backyard hunched in his poo position
squirting out little dribbles as he goes and nanc
and i cleaning up saying oh buddy you're making
this decision easier for us and we're not calling
to cancel now and he paces around outside and
in for hours till he finally lies down in his bed
and drops his head like he's sleeping but when
i look close i see his eyes are open open like
he's only going to close them one more time
and we go to work the next day and we have
people over to say goodbye to him and to us
all leaving to our separate destinations and
friday morning he is not making our job more
difficult with any kind of comeback in fact we
begin to wonder if he's going to make it to
his appointment that afternoon he stays in his

bed as nanc goes out to walk before dawn and
i sit down and work on this until i hear a squirting
sound behind me and then the smell and i follow
him around cleaning up the yellow pestilential
muck he is leaving behind it is like his insides
are dissolving and running out i finish a roll of paper
towels and get another i gag and retch and almost
puke i get it on my hands the little blobs are hard
to spot but you find them by the smell i have
mercifully to go to work so leave nanc with the
deathwatch and go to the lumberyard and
the job and i'm telling the carpenters what to do
and suddenly start crying tears falling in sawdust
and they stand around looking uncomfortable
till i get back in control and then i leave them to it
not really caring what they do and i'm driving around
thinking about T and thinking about this poem
how i have to keep this language game between
this way of thinking about it of keeping it there
but at the same time pushing it back because if i
don't push it back my insides will be dissolving
and i think about him walking ceaselessly around
the house head down and panting like he was
pulling the whole world behind him but he has
to do this one last thing he has to make it
to his appointment it is an obligation to us
and he will keep his obligation to his dying breath
but when i get back he is finally quiet and nanc
is sitting with him on the living room floor
crying saying she just walked him for the last

time and i lie down beside him put my face
in his neck and sob into the fur smell the good
dusty dogsmell and his dog-funky breath i want
to inhale him take him inside outside language
to feel him be real and he shifts a little and i
know he is uncomfortable and whatever i know
of him is absolutely human and that to be human
is to be incapable of knowing anything real
finally the time comes for his appointment and we
take him out to the car and help him in and it is
clouding up and i think there will be thunder
tonight but tonight renny is not going to be
afraid tonight the sky brings its terror
only to those who truly deserve it
and at nicole's office he's pulling at the leash
to go anywhere but through that door
just like he always did when he went to the vet
and just like always we pull him in and he wanders
around through the rooms and nicole says just
let him wander and she follows him and gives
him a shot of tranquilizer and she says this
will take about five minutes and then he's going
to get a little wobbly and then he's going
to pretty much sleep and then we'll give him
what is basically an overdose of sleeping pills
and he's walking around and nanc sitting on
the floor next to him when his legs fall
out from under him and then we're all
on the floor me and nanc and nicole and
then he's asleep but still won't close his eyes

while we cry and hug him and kiss him then
she puts the needle in the vein and a little
red rose of renny's blood blooms into the vial
and she pushes the plunger home

Tui

I found the place on google earth by searching for a circle
among the squares, like the perfect geometries one sees
flying over Texas, symmetries formed by the radial irrigators,
except here there is only the one circle, and tiny, among the
randomly defined rectangles of the small farms. And here
the circle is the roof of a simple yurt, the slightly conical roof
a tetilla among the fields.

The artist of this work is called Javier. Javier dresses simply,
like a workman, and drives a van, but his interest in the yurt
seems purely aesthetic. He shows us the rudiments of its
operation—how the locks work, how to open the shutters
on the big windows, how to get to the hipermercado,
paradoxically nearby—and then can't seem to get away
quickly enough, as if he can't bear to watch his creation
sullied by our backpacks and roll-aboards.

It's a single room, the bath area visually obscured by a curtain,
the bed behind a folding screen. I pace it off and calculate
the radius to be about five meters. The walls are clay tile,
the floors simulated wood, the ceiling plaster or stucco set
between radial beams, with a granite pole perhaps a foot in
diameter at the center.

This perfect circle is set within an irregular quadrangle

defined on two sides by the road and on the others by lush gardens of corn, greens and melon, hidden from view, once you are inside, by a curtain of dense bamboo, imported like us. The plot seems designed for nudists, for utter privacy, and we walk around naked, sometimes, with the farmers working just beyond the bamboo screen.

It's hard for us to judge if the people who live here and work these small farms have done so all their lives, inheriting the plots from previous generations of Galician farmers, or if they are transplants from elsewhere, having retired here to escape a former urban existence. The one who works the adjacent garden eyes us warily when he drives by on his tractor. We wave to him from the front gate, but he does not wave back. To him we are as alien, it seems, as the transplanted bamboo, and perhaps as pestilential.

Years ago, we were driving through the Czech Republic and had stopped for a night or two in the small village of Telc. In a pub the bartender asked me, practicing his English, "You are tourist?", less interested in fixing my identity than in understanding the concept of the tourist, as he probably didn't run into that many people who travelled without exigency, merely to be moving, observers for observation's sake. And I realized in the same moment that I didn't really understand the concept myself.

In Tui we tour the cathedral. On the floor of one of the capellas the marble is inscribed with names, the earliest one dated 1589. Beneath that floor are the bones of those who trampled the bones of a thousand others whose names are inscribed nowhere.

Dogs howl in the morning, vying with the roosters that are waking up all across our valley. We awake to this cacophony but then drift back to sleep, one day until almost noon. We are sad, worn out with loss. Birds, also, at dawn. There is one that makes an ugly, low-pitched squawk. They roost in the bamboo just outside the windows and torture us. Nanc says groggily, "hush up." I go stand in the window to see what they are, but all I can see are the shaking leaves. Then one flies by close in front of me with a noisy flutter of big wings. They are crow-sized, black with white markings. Magpies, I think.

There are moments I record here and moments I do not. Moments of terror or desire or shallow despair at the worthlessness of this endeavor. Why must I write? Because not to is to be a tourist.

My circular enclosure, the bamboo that has been planted specifically to shield me from the view of those who work the land.

Our friend—known, coincidentally, as T—comes with his lover to see us here in this place that is not ours. It's been a long time, fifteen years, since he moved to Korea to teach English. We've never met his lover and are worried, but it turns out we like him. Our friend, to our great surprise, is in Spain as a *peregrino*; he will take the rest of the summer to make the walk, the northern route, from Irun to Santiago de Compostela. We are taken aback by this turn toward the spiritual. Gay man from a Southern evangelical family, having endured the worst of what religious sects can dish out in terms of alienation, yet he returns to the tradition. Does he believe in God and heaven and hell, we ask. Well, heaven and hell not so much, he says.

Javier has decorated the yurt with several paintings and sculptures by "Nogue," which we are beginning to think is a pseudonym for himself, though who knows. He has stocked a small library also. An eclectic selection: *Antología Poética* of Rubén Dario; Antonio Blay's *La Realidad: Curso de Profundización y Diálogos*; and a ponderous *Alquimia & Mística* by Alexander Roob. To these I add, for future travelers, my own *Surrealismo*, bilingual, Enrique Solinas translation, and, in English, Tahar Djaout's *The Bone Seekers* and *A Passenger from the West*, by Nabile Farès. There is also a random collection of maps and information packets about nearby beaches and attractions. We want to go a little further, though, to Cangas, because Farès did.

Yesterday I swam in the river Minho (or Miño, if you are on the Spanish side.) At Monçao I got Nanc to hold my clothes while I jumped in and let the current take me a couple of hundred meters down the park. I saw a snake or perhaps some kind of eel in the shallows. The water is cold and the current strong yet manageable as long as you can touch bottom. I was walking along waist deep, however, and the bottom quite suddenly disappeared and did not come back.

After the first night's great sleep, last night I slept hardly at all, read Farès for a long time and then simply lay awake until I gave up and started writing around dawn.

Farès, writing about writing, imagines "—instead of my frightened and timid ballpoint—…an instant telescriber, an automatic." Prescient, perhaps, in 1970. Here and now, I have such a device at my fingertips but have no desire to use it. Writing to me is an activity that involves the fingers. It is a skill and a work that has little to do with the transcription of vocal language. Farès questions, also, the concept of "work," though it is unclear to me if he is using *travailler* or *oeuvre*, *trabajar* or *obrar*, a distinction we cannot make in English, without modification, a character not available on our keyboard.

Finally one of the birds leaves the squawking flock hidden in the foliage and roosts in the open just outside the window in front of me, and it is indeed a magpie, white streaks and the long tail. There is another voice among them, though, harsher and deeper, and I believe this is a bird I saw yesterday flying, at a distance, larger, with a topknot that gave it the look, in silhouette, of a pterodactyl.

I want to check the bird species, but the yurt is not connected to the internet. We have electricity, TV, water, air conditioning (which we don't use), but the lack of an internet connection seems like a great hardship. We spend time in silence, nap, read, talk… all with a fidgeting unease in the shadow, like the urge to smoke. I want to look up the birds, to make a dinner reservation, to check the spelling of *travailler* and the history of the Tui cathedral, to map the way to Cangas. No single entity (perhaps the closest would be the European church of the middle ages) has ever had as much sway over the human episteme as the google machine. Now, at the level of the species, all truth resides in its texture.

Tonight, a strange dream. I am lying in the bed, this exact bed, in Tui, and my arm touches something beside me in the dark. I feel around the fleshy shape and realize with horror that it is my father's head, that he has collapsed on the floor beside me and is leaning his head against the side of the mattress. I scream for my mother whom, it seems, is sleeping beside me, but my scream is siphoned off into the silence of the dream. I realize, then, that I am dreaming and that I must wake myself in order to save my father, so I try with all my might to make a real scream out of the dream scream. I finally succeed in making a tiny grunt with my actual voice, and I come back to myself beside Nanc in this bed in this yurt among the farms. I lie in the dark awake. Far away, across the valley, dogs are faintly howling. I negotiate with myself as to whether or not to get up and write this. I rather don't want to because we are going to Cangas tomorrow and I don't want to be tired. But I roll words over and over in my mind until I do, finally, get up and write this, which is not what I had imagined at all.

In this dream, there is an element that has appeared in my dreams since I was very young, sleeping in my room across the hall from my parents. The recurrent element has nothing to do with the quasi-oedipal content, which seems almost too obvious, as if it were some kind of feint, a parody of a revelation. The repeated, generic feature of this dream is the realization that I am dreaming and the attempt, against the paralysis of sleep, to wake myself, which I always just manage to do. Over the course of five decades I have woken myself from such urgent-seeming dreams, nightmares, perhaps a thousand times, and yet it has taken me this long to realize that the matter of my dreams is probably insignificant beside this structural motif, and that this structure, this terror at the very fact that I am dreaming, is the intimation of my death, the dream from which I will not awaken.

This writing, this act of writing, also recurrent since I was a teenager, resembles this dream in that the content is always arbitrary, symbolic, full of feints and false clues, and my effort, always, is to awaken from it, to write beyond the writing into a realm where writing no longer enthralls, which is the awakening into death.

We go into Tui this morning for breakfast and internet, and I wish we hadn't, as the news there is horrible, yet more tidings of irretrievable loss, this time from an unexpected sector of my life: the drummer in my band is moving away, leaving the bass player and me to either call it quits or find another drummer and besides that leaving me minus one dear friend. This news saddens me more than I want to admit and colors our drive to Cangas. I'm sad almost to the point of tears and compensate by being an ass; we argue about directions, turn-offs, etc., and when we finally get there, park and begin wandering the beach—all but empty due to the chilly, overcast day—I begin to feel like a tourist, having come to this place where I do not belong merely to observe.

We walk along the boardwalk reading the menu-del-día's and finally decide on a place for lunch. We sit *afuera* and gradually, as the white wine and courses of fish and shellfish flow, strike up a conversation with two women at the next table. They are Rosa and Maria José, government workers from central Galicia, here on holiday, for the 14th time. They are staying at Cabohome, a few kilometers away, where the water and the views, they say, are much better than here in Cangas, and the beach is nude. I struggle to speak and to understand as Nanc and they chatter. They're impressed with Nanc's Spanish and happily tolerant of mine. They want us to come to Cabohome and hang on the nude beach with them. Rosa gets up, pulls up her shirt and down her jeans to show me the lack of tan line. She sees something, she says, in my eyes, a calm, a nobility, or something. She tries out the English word; "eyes" she says, looking into them.

We are all quite drunk by the time the dessert courses are done, and we hug and kiss good-bye full of promises that we'll see them at Cabohome tomorrow. Then Nanc and I go down to the beach. She gathers beach glass, prolific here, while I go into the frigid water, the only swimmer on the beach, wanting to sober up a bit before the drive home. The sand is khaki-colored and coarse, and the water is clear. When I dive under and open my eyes, I feel nothing. I tell Nanc that the water must have the exact salinity of tears. "Are you crying?" she says.

Back in the yurt, neither of us want dinner. We watch the news and weather, crisis in Catalonia, new leadership coming for the PP, sunny in Galicia tomorrow. We drink a bottle of tinto and I puff on my vape, then, at dusk, we take a walk around the neighborhood. We are on a mountainside and the farms are terraced, the roads ancient and crooked, sometimes fenced with granite walls on both sides. There are lots of dogs who harangue us viciously as we walk by. At one house, a formidable German Shepherd appears at the top of the wall above us and seems ready to jump down, but we pretend disinterest and walk on.

It is 10:30 but barely dark when we go to bed. I read a little in the Farès but end up spending most of the night lying silently half awake. Every so often a dog will start up in the distance and twenty others around the valley will take up the cry. Finally the birds let me know that dawn has arrived, and I open my eyes.

Today we go up the mountain, just outside Tui, to the Parque Natural de Monte Aloia, a tricky drive up switchbacks through the dense bosque. At the top there is an old chapel; monks seem to have arrived everywhere before anyone else. Everything is built out of granite, which also forms the forest floor, dirt of the region, great boulders covered with thick moss and ferns. At the top of the *monte* we discover, somewhat though not entirely to our surprise, a *taperia*, and though we have brought a picnic for ourselves we decide to try it. We haven't yet had tortilla on this trip, and the friendly waitress recommends the *empanada de bacalhao*, so we have all that, plus a bottle of the *vinho branco de la casa*, always speaking something that hovers in a nexus among Spanish, Portuguese and Gallega.

The white wine is so delicious we ask for a bottle *para llevar. Es posible? Sí claro!* And then we drive back down the mountain, following the paper map the park guide has given us, looking for the bottom of the little river (*río Deique*), where we have heard there is a pool suitable for swimming.

The place is normally got to afoot and the driving path is lengthy and circuitous, and we miss it on the first pass, each accusing the other of poor navigation, interpretation of map signs and road signs. Finally I turn, over Nanc's objection, off the highway onto a dirt road that leads, in a mere 200 meters, to the *laguito* we are looking for. The place is gorgeous, a mill pond (the ancient mill enclosure is still there) of crystal clear runoff from the mountain above, dammed to a depth of about 5 feet, the surface dotted with tiny blossoms from the trees which overhang it all around, indistinguishable from the dotting of the same blossoms on the bottom.

As I approach the dam a small brown snake, a *culebra* from the park brochure, streaks into the water and swims, on the surface, to the other side, where it disappears into the dense grass on the shore. We are alone here but for this one snake and whatever else might be peeking out of the vegetation, and I get naked (but for my sandals; the bottom is rocky) and jump in. The water is freezing, colder even than the ocean, snow-melt fallen down from frigid heights, filtered through the continuous skein of ferns and grasses into this basin where it is invisible but for its reflective surface, cold glass where I see my aging naked self for an instant before crashing into it.

The cold means less to me now than it did when I was younger. I know the cold but also a numbness to it, bearing it from a certain distance, as if esomeone else were feeling the cold and describing it to me.

Nanc gets naked and gets in too, for a moment, shivering. Then we both get out and spread towels in the grass and settle down to nap. We're drunk from the wine at the *taperia* and have started on the extra bottle we bought, and we lie down naked in the forest. I take a few pulls from the vape and settle into an opium dream in the dreamy afternoon, caught up in the day—a term which stands, equally, for the hours of that particular day, the historic displacements of recent wars, and the restraints and currencies negotiated or stolen by generations past—as if in a pair of cupped palms, and we fall asleep in that great stoned green granite cathedral.
I wake up a little later, put on my boots and leave Nanc sleeping while I wander in the woods, hoping to find another *culebra* or perhaps one of the salamanders or frogs we've seen in the illustrations. I don't, but following the stream upriver it is so lovely I break down and take some pictures on my phone, thinking what a nice spread they'll make on Facebook. In this edenic wilderness I come across only one piece of litter: a small piece of paper on which is written, in neat cursive: *"comando caca."*

Returning, sobered, to the writing in the early morning as the magpies squawk and rustle the bamboo just outside the big open windows. Roosters, too, are crowing in the distance. A tractor chugs by on the road. I record these details without knowing why.

One summer, I believe it was in 2000, after working the study abroad program in Prague for the month of July, we rented a car in Prague and drove down to Croatia for our vacation. After almost two weeks on the road we returned to Prague, dropped off the car, and had one night to spend before the flight home. Thinking it would be the cheapest and easiest thing, we went back to the dorm we had spent the previous month in. We had good memories of the place. It had a pub in the basement where we had nightcaps almost every night with the students (there were about 100 of them) and other teachers. So the girl at the front desk knew us and gave us the same room we had had for the month, and we drug our bags down the empty hallway that had bustled with life every morning before class. We got into the room, noting how empty and quiet everything felt now, and then went down to the pub. The big room, where we used to have to ask people to move to make room for a dart game, was empty but for the bartender. We got our beers and sat down, but the place depressed both of us terribly. It seemed dead in a more than metaphorical way, not only empty but empty as awakening into emptiness, revealing that its former fullness was illusion, a dream.

More and more, life feels emptied out like that. A particular activity—teaching, the band, etc.—comes to an end and with that end comes the realization that it had never possessed the fullness I had imagined it had. Increasingly, I am a tourist at someone else's activity, someone else's work. As Mark's title *Tourist at a Miracle* suggests, I may be witnessing some sort of great work, but it is not happening to or through me. "The young in one another's arms…", etc., and for some reason, unlike everyone else I know, I seem to be unable to rationalize a happy end or some sort of purpose to it. I may "finally have time to write" but unfortunately the writing itself is not immune to the spreading grayness.

Writing has become (or was it always?) a cliquish activity, small groups of writer/readers who read only other writer/readers like themselves, of similar age and proclivity. Writing, which set out (in Farès, for example) to be a reclamation of identity, has become, inexorably, the new delineation of exile. If I am sailing to Byzantium, what should I expect to find there but guided tours and souvenirs?

This morning the dogs are silent. This requires a delicate balance, an entire ecosystem walking on tiptoe, because the least suspicion by any single dog will set the entire valley off. The roosters start crowing while it is still completely dark and continue as the daylight gradually comes to. I lie awake and observe all this until I finally rise again and come to the writing. I work for less than an hour then get sleepy again and go back to bed. There is nothing to say, after all; there are only these images of aging and dawn to be continuously elaborated and embellished.

Earth, says Farès, is composed of air, eggs and tea. What he means here is that once you invite language into the room you have no choice but to follow its metonymies and metaphors to the very end, when Twilight drinks up the Earth and both find their resolution, Twilight in satisfying her thirst, Earth in being drunk up. My argument (by which I mean my hope and unfounded faith) is that a little bit of dawn and magpie squawking spills out the corners of his mouth and dribbles over this valley of the *río Minho*, so that Twilight ends up swallowing nothing but itself, yet again. Maybe the streamers of meaning we imagine the metonymy drags behind it don't make it into night's maw before it snaps shut and cuts them off like scraps of spaghetti or the little eels (*gulas*) I ate last night (is it me that is the Twilight? is this enormous figure I keep discovering only my own shadow?).

Our final dinner is in Valença, at the first place across the old bridge, a peregrino stop. Lovely *vinho verde* (*tinto*, oddly enough) and a *tabúa do quiejo*, with *lomo*. In the morning we leave for Lisbon, where we'll stay in the airport hotel and fly back Tuesday morning.

"*Poesia não basta,*" reads a fresh bit of graffiti down in Baixa, near the train station.

Return

so we're dogsitting lou the other night and
i wake up about 3:30 to barking or actually
a kind of howling or wailing from the front room
and i'm thinking how strange because
you know how lou is she'll sit for hours

at the door waiting for someone to happen by
and open it and never bark never make a sound
so i thought something must be going on
maybe some drunk from pal's on the front porch
and thinking i ought to go check i sit up
and when i swing my feet off the bed
i put them down right on lou she is sleeping
just under me back against the bed like
she likes to do and perfectly still and quiet
and i feel that chill like i felt when after mama died
i was staying at the old house and she brushed
by me in the hall one night and the hair on the
back of my neck stood up and half afraid half
curious i step over lou who doesn't even wake
up and i go up front and stand in the living
room dark but for the street light through the window
and sort of see and sort of remember you standing
at the door nose against the crack like you
always did when someone was on the porch
and then the vision fades and i am alone
again in the dim silent room and sad thinking
there will come a day when nanc is walking
by herself for she still walks in the morning
just by herself now there will come a day
when she runs into neighbors and none
of them will ask about you and make
her cry again there will come a day when
when i get home from work and put my key
in the door i don't feel your absence inside
and even your ghost will have dissolved into

the routine of thoughts and days and i keep
staring at the door wanting to feel that
chill again but you don't reappear because
you can't will such things and i go back
to bed and lou is still there sound asleep
and nanc still sleeping on the other side
as i lay back down and wonder if maybe i am
still asleep too and dreaming like i sometimes
do for i have been dreaming and wake up
and then later wake up again like that for many
years the first when i was young so young i was
still afraid of the dark i woke up from a nightmare
and reached for the bedside lamp but when
i turned on the switch nothing happened
and i fumbled in the dark to find the cord
and run my hand down it till i find the end
unplugged and feel along the wall till i find
the outlet and try to plug it back in in the dark
but the prongs have gone rubbery and wiggle
and bend and will not go in so i get up and
go downstairs and outside to my bike
and take off down sang street turning on
the headlight but nothing happens and then
reaching forward feeling for the headlight only
to find it missing and duct tape over the hole
like a drum head so i ride on through the dim
night motor rumbling under me and head
into town where the streets are lit questing for
light and heading down maple in front of the old
student union i come upon a wreck there are

cop cars and blue lights flashing and in the middle
a broken car which as i pass i realize is my
own the station wagon work car my parents
let me use at night and my father is there
talking to the cops he had had a load of baseball
bats in the back and they have spilled out onto
the street and i ride by and i'm surprised and sort
of worried to see him there but he doesn't see
me and i keep on going and avert my eyes
and about then i wake up again this time
assumedly for real but there is a funny thing
about this dream this dream i had forty years
ago but has haunted ever since this dream
that i have written in poems and journals
and told to three different analysts this dream
that was the first of hundreds of dreams
in which i dream i wake up but then wake up again
and the funny thing is that in all these
writings and tellings and analyses i missed
a connection which i just noticed just now
and that is something about my uncle joe
you never met my uncle joe my father's brother
for he died before you were born but if you
had you might have mistaken him for me
for he looked just like my old man and i
look just like he did at my age uncle
joe was my father's only brother who lived
to adulthood though they had four sisters
and he was the only one of the siblings who
made it as they say he had an electronics

business in texarkana and a big house and
three brand new cars and a private plane
and he had four sons one of whom jim
was my age and my parents used to put me
on the train in siloam springs and send me
down to stay with them for a week or so
in the summer i loved those visits they
lived a life that was exotic luxury compared
to mine for the boys never had to work in the
summer and we could stay up late and watch
tv or read comic books and sleep as late as we
wanted and play board games or pool all day
and once he even took us flying when he was
going down to lubbock to check on one of his
stores and he let me sit in the copilot seat
and steer the little cessna for a few minutes
he let jim and the others do whatever they
wanted and took them flying all the time and
bought them cars and/or motorcycles as soon
as they turned sixteen so i could never under-
stand why jim hated him i hate his fucking
guts jim used to say to me but there was this
thing that happened once when i was staying
there i woke up early and had to pee so i
got up and went into the bathroom they
had that kind of bathroom that was between
two bedrooms and opened into the parents'
room on one side and the boys' room on the other
and when i opened the door on this morning
uncle joe was standing there naked at the sink

and i was mortified and closed the door as
quick as i could but he opened it back up
now with a towel around him and he said
no no it's ok come on in and i said no no
i can wait and ran back to the bed and the other
thing is that uncle joe coached a little league
baseball team lavender electronics jim
was on it and sometimes they would practice
while i was there and i would go with
jim and uncle joe to the park in the station
wagon and in the back of the station wagon
there was always a bunch of bats
along with other stuff like bases and catcher's
gear always a load of bats that rolled around
as the station wagon turned this way and that
and then a decade later i have this dream
that will haunt me the rest of my life
about those stupid bats and just now as i
say it i see a swarm of bats flying out of
a cave mouth that sort of pun i imagine
would not be accessible to you unless of course
there is a particular barking sound that might
mean in one case for example i'm going to bite
you if you come closer and in another context
feed me please please please or something like
that i do know dogs dream because i've seen
your legs twitching in your sleep and heard the faint
noises in your throat once i even woke you
because you seemed to be having a nightmare
and you lifted your head with a start and

stared at me and i wonder if you remembered
that dream and if it continued to haunt you
with images of bats and bats or of the rough
skin of the tree trunks and the plosives that came
from your throat questions for scientists i suppose
maybe a psychologist with an mri of your head
could see which cells are lighting up when you bark
or when you think about bark maybe one day they'll
be able to light up the path that leads from uncle
joe's dick to a cloud of bats leaving their cave
and talk about it on npr i was thumbing
through old photos on facebook and came
on several of you one in bed with nanc your head
on my pillow one with joseph lying beside you
and it looks like you are hugging him
and i'm pleased to report that i was able to
look at these images without crying so i guess
i have reached that point where as people
say it is "getting better" and i also haven't
been running into your ghost so much around
the house lately but i wonder if that is
because you're actually gone or if
you're still here and i have just lost
your channel maybe i am the one gone
blind walled up in my house as far
from you as your bark from its tree
and the last time i had one of those
dreams and got scared and was
trying to wake myself it occurred to me
that maybe there wasn't anything

to be afraid of here maybe i just
needed to let the dream take me
where it will and so i tried that

Time

the last time i saw tim except
for a couple of quick
visits where i was passing
through boston or he was
passing through here must have
been 30 years at least but
i had heard he'd remarried or at
least re-hooked-up and retired
and re-divorced or re-broke-up
and finally moved back
to little rock where he'd never
in a million years imagined he
would end up and i asked
if any of the old gang was
still there and he said there
were two or three but they
were all doing stuff and busy
and not the same anymore anyway
so he was trying to meet people
not that easy when you don't have
work to sort of force the issue
and chuck said yeah i don't have
that problem because he's working
at lowes now and his days are all
paint paint and pain he said
(because of his knee) though
the people he worked with were
nice and we said oh that's good

and tim said he'd been to dallas
to see richard and jan and
we asked how they were how's
jan doing and he said she was
doing well improving every
day though of course
there were lasting effects partial
paralysis on one side her left
hand curled and her mouth
gone slack so it was difficult
for her to eat they'd gone
out to dinner and richard
had to cut up her food etc.
so while it was nice getting
out it was kind of a lot of
trouble and it was they said
normally just easier
to stay home and richard
had said at first he was thinking
maybe a year and then he started
saying maybe two years and then
had come to the realization that
the doctors were saying maybe
this long maybe that long
just to keep them hoping and it
was finally starting to wear
on him richard even indomitable
richard and he was looking back
on his work on his thousands
of negatives and prints the art

he had devoted his life to and
now wondering what exactly he'd
done it for the community
college where he'd been for 35
years had given him a great
darkroom all he'd ever hoped for
and then one day it was out of
date and they made the trans-
ition to digital and chuck said
yeah there's a big show right now
at the ogden you should check
it out if you have time for museum
hopping while you're here it's
really big hundreds of prints
and there are maybe two
silver prints in the whole thing
and it's actually pretty hard
to pick them out the digital printing
is getting so good and i said
yeah it's the same in the print
world the digital stuff has changed
everything like i hear people all
the time worrying about e-books
but i tell them the real
change has been in print
technology like when i started
out with this idea of being
a poet publishing a book was
a really big deal now anyone
can publish a book i have

a dozen and who cares and tim gave me
that look he's always given me
like he's trying to figure out
what it is that makes me tick
like he's never really understood
just like i've never really under-
stood him and then he and chuck
both thought they'd better go
(it was like 8) since nanc and i
were flying tomorrow so we all hugged
goodnight and tim said to nanc
whom he'd only met the one time
before when we were passing through
boston thanks so much for the del-
icious dinner i had heard you
were a great cook and i see
it's true and have a great time
in boulder and say hi to ben
and i almost said yeah we're going
to see your godson but caught myself
trying to remember if it was him
or chuck who was ben's godfather
and the other one was will's
and then i remembered a little
flash popped up in my head it was
chuck saying "my ben" that's the flash
that always reminds me which of them
is which son's godfather and then
they left and the last thing
i heard as they were walking

down the steps is tim saying
to chuck can i drop you? and i didn't
hear the answer they always had
a bit of a thing always a bit
closer to each other than with me
at least that's what i imagined
even back in the 80s when the 3
of us were pretty tight and in
the band and going to punk shows
three or four nights a week
and i went in to help
nanc clean up but it was all done
she'd washed every dish while we'd
been yapping and i felt bad
about it but the truth is she said
she wasn't all that fascinated
by our trips down memory lane
and then we did christmas eve
gifts i picked out her pajamas
from under the tree and she said
they looked big but when she
tried them on they fit and she
said yeah large is what i
wear and she gave me two
pair of sweat pants one light
for summer one fleece lined
they fit great great for yoga
and for lounging and then we went
to bed and i lay there awake like
i always do now read a little and

then lay there some more couldn't
stop thinking about richard and jan
richard who'd come to fayetteville
in 1970 and enrolled pre-med
at his father's insistence but
changed his major to art
then went on to grad school
at the institute in chicago
richard who was always
so sure of himself and where
he was going and what he was
doing it was hard for me to
imagine him disillusioned he and jan
had met in undergrad and moved
in together and been together ever
since and i remembered that time
we had been drinking on dickson
street me and richard and jan and
deb and we were walking over to
deb and my place to smoke a joint
drunk and happy running in the steet
and at one point jan and i sort of
ran into each other behind a truck
out of sight of the others and we
kissed grabbed each other and
kissed one of those kisses
i felt in every pore like she was
flowing through me and when we got
to our place i wanted her so badly
i was blushing and panting couldn't

speak but she sat down cool as
could be and started telling
a story like nothing had happened
at all and we never spoke of that
kiss nor repeated it and i thought
of her now with her hand curled up
and richard cutting up her food
and the strange thing was when i
got up and started writing this
i was going to call it tim but
it came out time every time
i typed tim in this whole long
rambling poem-thing written
before dawn this christmas 2018
for god knows what reason
every time i typed tim's name
my left middle finger shot
out of its own accord and added
the e and i had to correct
reminds me of a tic i used to have
where every time i typed my name
at the bottom of an email it came
out boill and i thought it must have
been some kind of symptom
some unconscious problem i had
with my name took me
years to get over it

Lisa's House, Boulder

inside lisa's house
nested in this
quaint old-town
neighborhood in
boulder there is
on the wall a picture
of that same house
in 1898 sitting
by itself
in a field
of snow
blank but
for a barn barely
visible in the distance
and i wondered if
that house had
on its wall
a picture of itself
that much older
solitary
on the barren ice
and perhaps that one
too had a picture
of lisa's house
in empty space
lisa's house utterly
alone in the universe

Of Dreaming

——

something shifts
in the superstructure
landscape
bumping softly

——

how can we hold responsible
speakers for what they say
or dreamers for what they dream?
you can't
have your freud
and eat jung too

——

what codec
is reality?

——

is the dream
the report of the dream?
perhaps not—
perhaps the dream
        is the dream
and the report

another dream

＝

what is this fallen
other we call we?
not we who use the word
from our ethical high horse,
                        certainly

＝

my friend
is a babbling brook
run-on
without cessation

＝

I just saw an excellent
clown outfit
in my dream

＝

after this
only blank pages
and what
surface will they skim?

＝

I'm after a poem

there is no way to
talk about
like a dream
you can't describe

———

the way the words
slip between trees

———

what a commotion
the cat makes
at midnight
outside
pushing to be
let in
like a dream

———

try to tell the simple truth
and the repressed slips
out in the accident
but try to tell the truth
of a dream and the repressed
is manifest
in silence

＝

in dreams we
work out the problems of reality
and in reality we
work out the problems of
dreams

＝

newspaper article on dreams:
    "looking for an inexpensive
    path to self-knowledge?"
ouija boards and crystal balls:
this is the self

＝

I dream
there's a stain
on my leg and
it won't come off

＝

the world is our desire
reflected we are
responsible for what
happens in the world
as we are for what happens
in our dreams

＝

what's surprising
isn't that Jung discovered
archetypes but
that he was surprised to

＝

after the storm
the city is flooded
I am wading
in the water
a beautiful day
the water
crystal clear
fish swim around my ankles
green grass waving in the current

＝

Dream tricks:
1. Just before sleep, re-
mind yourself to pay attention
and try to remember your dreams.
2. On waking, don't
immediately get up and start
your day but think back on the dream,
reconstruct it in your mind.
3. Write it down as quickly as possible.

I am sitting in my office, engrossed in my writing on the computer screen, when I notice that someone else is in the room. I turn and see not only the one person whose movement had caught my eye but a whole crowd milling about. They are teenagers and seem utterly oblivious to the fact that they have interrupted me at my work. I stand up and shout at them to get their attention. They stop talking and all turn to look at me.

"What are you doing here?" I say.

They shift about uncomfortably for a moment before one of them offers that Russell (my stepson, apparently) has invited them to a party. But I do not see Russell.

"Where is Russell? Who let you in?"

They all look around as if they cannot remember, or they mumble unintelligibly.

I decide that I may be able to find Russell if I can trace back the train of admitters to the first one, so I turn to a girl standing near me and ask her specifically who let her in. She points to a girl sitting on the sofa. I go to her and ask her the same question, and she says, "Steve."

I look around the room and yell, "Steve!" Another girl says that he has gone downstairs to play pool. I go to the top of the stairs and call his name again. I can hear the pool balls colliding in the basement, and a voice in answer. I tell him to come up and talk to me, and I hear footsteps on the stairs. I turn from the stairs back to the room, only to find that all the other kids have disappeared without a trace. Apparently I made them uncomfortable enough that they elected to slip out rather than face more of my interrogation. I turn back to the stairwell just in time to see a form just exiting around the corner: Steve has made his exit as well.

Growing somewhat nervous, and uncertain whether I am alone in the house or not, I walk down the bedroom hallway. The door to Russell's room is open. I can see only the foot of his bed and a pair of feet protruding from the covers.

I hear a noise and look down to the end of the long hallway, where I see a glass door. Beyond this door I see several people bustling about as if at work. An official, authoritative looking woman hurries along with another, younger woman at her side, to whom she appears to be dictating orders. The younger woman follows at a trot, occasionally stopping to write in her notepad.

I leave the hallway and go to the front door. The door opens onto a wide porch on which several groups of people are now seated at tables, apparently awaiting their breakfast, even though it is not yet dawn. It is quite dark on the porch. They have to squint in dim candlelight or light matches to read the menus.

The hostess comes up and looks at me questioningly.

"Isn't it awfully early for breakfast?" I ask.

"Well," she says, "a lot of them are here to stay. And, you know, the hand that's had a slight moves quickly."

====

she tugs
on my foot
to wake me,

"do you still have
your headache?"

====

the dream is
the hope the longing
for a dream to come
also the terror
that it might come

====

if life is just a dream
it is sad illusion
but if
life is a dream
it is happy and true
we dream
these onlys and justs

====

what kind of
people are we
who drift into easy
sleep leaving our
children to fend
on the rubbish pile?

═

I answer
the door
and dream someone
filling the opening
like a mirror—
it's Miroslav

═

putting on that
nonchalant air
carefully constructing
emptiness
brick by brick

═

do films resemble dreams
or do dreams resemble film?
did Disney
teach us to dream?

═

some people we
love but
barely remember
talking outside the window
keeping us awake

＝

what wish isn't
a death wish?
what wish isn't
to be released
from the dream?

＝

a coxcomb
a sail
a slight swale

＝

the crooked scarred
track of meaning:
where would we be
without meaning
to be there?

＝

i have to ask
what color is
your bonnet
your
other

＝

THIS seems to be no

more than it seems, its
truth obvious in mere appearance.
THIS, on the other hand,
is definitely more,
yields more
the deeper we dig.

══

dreaming in tandem
dreaming while
the city fills with smoke
dreaming
of spokes

══

We read
dreams as prophetic
and reality as expository
but this difference
is only context.

══

What strides we've
made in the past century
in terms of image:
imagine: a Muybridge sequence
from his own chemical processes
to the stable full of workers
coding for Adobe.

Image-making is
the image of all we've accomplished,
and all we will.

=====

image in the blood
declined
in hemoglobin

=====

thunk of a
high-voltage switch
kicking on
and then the hum

Of Sighing

The last sigh, your sigh, dies with me, this long alas! alas! sighed upon
me, the last woe-begotten Oedipus.
    —Nietzsche, *Philosophy and Truth*

If this is truth, it is not the truth that seems at first sight to be expressed
by these words. It's less a theory than a sigh.
    —Wittgenstein, *Culture and Value*

Religion is the sigh of the oppressed creature, the heart of a heartless
world, the soul of a soulless condition.
    —Marx, Critique of Hegel's *Philosophy of Right*

What do you do when you resign yourself to your fate? That's right,
you sigh. Every animal does. Take a horse. He sighs by smacking his lips
while wetting them with this tongue. You just gotta know how to read
em. And that's hard to learn living 50 stories up in concrete and steel.
    —*Hey Pup, Fetch It Up!: The Complete Retriever Training Book*

A fox and a monkey were on the road together, and fell into a dispute as
to which of the two was the better born. They kept it up for some time,
till they came to a place where the road passed through a cemetery
full of monuments, when the monkey stopped and looked about him
and gave a great sigh. "Why do you sigh?" said the fox. The monkey
pointed to the tombs and replied, "All the monuments that you see here
were put up in honor of my forefathers, who in their day were eminent
folk. The fox was speechless for a moment, but quickly recovering he
said, "Oh! don't stop at any lie, sir; you're quite safe: I'm sure none of
your ancestors will rise up and expose you."
Boasters brag most when they cannot be detected.
    —Aesop

＝

sigh of relief
sigh of exasperation
sigh of contentment
sigh of resignation

sigh of melancholy
sign of amazement
sigh of irritation
sigh of tenderness

sigh that says "Yes, there's nothing
left for you and me but to sip sweet wine, my dear,
now that the time has come for these young ones
to be thus boldly, provocatively happy."

sigh of hope
sigh of nostalgia
sigh of happiness at the pleasure
you will likely never experience again

found sigh
sigh overheard
sigh forgotten
repeated sigh

sigh of pleasure
sigh of death
sigh of return
sigh of release

⹀

The dog gets in bed with me before dawn.
He lies down beside me and I put my arm
across his chest and my face into the fur
on his nape. He inhales to maximum
extension, holds the breath for a moment,
then exhales forcefully and with slight
pharyngeal friction, producing a low almost
inaudible moan.

⹀

I'm not getting the job.
So nice to just lay back.
The espresso machine is broken.
Oh christ, another flat tire.

I guess I'd better pass.
What a wonderful lazy day.
Just sold the last one.
We would have been so good together.

They make great pets but don't live that long.
No paper this morning.
Oh that's such excellent news.
Ah that first cool breath of fall.

⹀

Is a sigh a word?

Is it a sign?
Is it learned
like a word
or are we born
sighing?
Does it pass from
body to body, breath
to breath, like a yawn?
Does it have a history,
etymology back to the dawn
of time, and even beyond,
since animals also sigh
and yawn?

⸻

I heard the dog sigh
when I was not in the room
just as I sometimes speak
when no one else
is in the room,
as now.

⸻

Can a sigh
be a lie?
Can it be ironic?
Sarcastic?
A parody?

═

The sigh is the sign
of the sign's
inability to sign,
sign of hunger
in satiety, anger
in love, confusion
in lucidity, what is left
wanting when all that was
wanted has been attained.
Sigh is the sign
that signs are not more
than the breath exhaled
in their making.

═

What does the dog mean
when she sighs?
You can read all 2000
pages of Poyatos's
Nonverbal Communication
and not get one whit
closer to an answer.

═

When it thunders, even if
(perhaps mostly when) the thunder
is distant, the fiercest dog

is terrified and cowers
under a chair. Fear of the privation
a storm can bring (ie death)
surfaces dumbly through the species.
Humans, on the other hand,
live with the certainty of death
every moment of every day
and spend their entire existence
trembling beneath a chair.

====

A sigh for self love:
it only happens when the self
is imagined (constructed,
configured, costumed, concocted)
as something the self desires,
something explicitly not
the self.

====

To examine sighing
is to pick one grain
of sand from the shore,
describe it, draw it,
obsess over it, fall
in love with it.

====

If we didn't have the word "sigh"

would the activity itself disappear?
The evolution not of sighing
but of the word which denotes it
is the evolution of sighing.

═══

Hysterical past
giving way
to arrogant presence.

Writer's Retreat (Marginalia)

This shell to protect me
while I
work some things out.

=

Parataxis: not a technique but
the representation itself.

=

Ceiling fan turning
cross and gyre
in the dull evening light.

=

A simple single thread
that turns back on itself
again and again
and becomes a knot.

=

We write to make
the absent present
and vice versa.

=

A star sent out

that light we see tonight
a million years before humans existed
and after.

———

To turn over a new leaf.
To become a leaf
trembling in the wind.

———

Motor purring quietly outside
then pulling away. Distant voices.
Someone walking
on the wooden floor next door.

———

All language
is apostrophe.

———

Whatever I say, invert.
Proscription is prescription.
Unity is division.
Etc.

———

I can say I but
if you'd rather

I can disappear:
it is an *aesthetic decision*.

====

The risk isn't discovering
you have nothing to say
but that you aren't there to say it.

====

The old wooden fence
weathered, green algae
starting up from the bottom.
When a gust hits
the pecan tree
nuts hit the tin roof hard.
I lie down stoned
and feel this as touch,
as if I went all the way out.

====

The billionaire and the terrorist wake
every morning with the same
lust for revenge.

====

World is a rebus.
Picture yourself
here in this text.

====

Why if I am to be
reconciled with death
should it be in writing?

====

I built you;
can you contain me?
You, with your porch
and your garret,
your recesses and your mice.

====

Procedural writing,
writing according to rules,
feels like a narrowing down,
but taking decisions away
from the unconscious
actually widens the field.
Thus this narrow path.

====

Language 1:
The self alone with God
(or nothingness), space of prayer
from inner depths, the soul.
Language 2:
Self absolutely social,

intersubjective, populated
by others, pure mimicry,
automism.

=

That ache beyond wound
or hunger that resides at the center
of a perfect spring day.
If this suffering could be alleviated,
would the other kinds also?

=

Beating time
to being.
For the time being
being.

=

That grand importance
of heritage, blood—
it is a text that teaches us this.

=

Why the polemical
stand against division?
What is gained
from unity?

=

A storm, long anticipated,
has arrived. Dead calm.
The eye of something.

=

As if the letters themselves
might vie with death, infect
it from the inside, kill it.

=

Is there anything more
hideous than a Hollywood smile?
And every smile
is a Hollywood smile.

=

That playful, aggressive
spirit of youth, mock
combat of sports, evolving
finally into (a) real animosity or
(b) lifelong friendship.

=

The dream is a rebus.
Picture me there and
pay what you owe.

=

These delicate ways of wording
are of no benefit in speech.
Rhetoric is stand-in for the body.

=

The constrictor squeezes.
You breathe out.
It squeezes a little more.

=

Plato sees the psychology of the individual
reflected in the politics of the city.
Thus the Symposium, if you
haven't noticed, is an orgy.

=

If you look up at the tree
you will fear it falling
as indeed someday it will,
but lie down in its roots and arms....

=

Recording, in a manner of speaking,
the gulf between halting uncertain
speech and the soon-to-come
fluidity of the writing.

People who are always
upbeat and happy
aren't.

———

Quintillian and Cicero imagine
they are prescribing strategies
for verbal combat,
but in fact they chant
dreams in a trance
like the shamans of old.

———

Birds taking flight.
I flew into a tree.

———

As I wake from a nap my dream
hovers at arm's length, postage stamp
square of image and text, too far away
and poorly lit for these failing eyes to read.

———

"The measure of language is its use."
But "use" implies will, a speaker's mastery
(and speech of a Master)
as well as a further purpose.

What of language that erupts?
The slur, the slip, the swear?
What if language were not a thing we use
but a thing we are used by?
The measure of language is it's us.

＝＝

To have an aesthetic is already an ideological decision.
There is no "right wing" art.
Even the work that attempted to be that
(Pound, Dalí, Marinetti) was ignored by the right
and then co-opted—in brackets, with redactions—
by the left.

＝＝

Our critiques of the Other…
Hypocrite is not, etymologically,
hypo-critical, but an actor,
lines preordained,
not to be argued with
except by another actor.

＝＝

At St. Elizabeth's Pound bragged
that the Pisan Cantos had come
to him in one ecstatic rush,
but they later uncovered
multiple early drafts.
What image of the

authorial self requires
composition to be spontaneous?
What defensive anxiety
does this lie assuage?

===

The woman walking in front of me turns
around, sensing my eyes on her.
We are all together, all sense
together in the single
network of desire.

===

Ant hive functioning as a single
organism or a school of fish
turning at the same moment,
but no animal is more fully
linked to the tribe,
no subject more intimately
intersubjective than the human.

===

No matter how I try to isolate
myself, there you are, looking
over my shoulder.

===

Would it be better, more authentic,

to make this appeal in speech
rather than writing? Speaking to you,
perhaps, or an imagined you.
Or speaking quietly to myself.
Or simply thinking.

═══

The lush gardens of early summer.
That heavy, humid heat that weighs
on everything as it strives
to get out of the ground.

═══

I keep forgetting that word "muscadine."

═══

Who is a master of language?
It's like saying, "I can swim, therefore
I am master of the ocean.
The waves move at my will."

═══

Something you can bet on:
Whenever there is inexplicable
mischief—a lamp knocked over,
a hole in the screen edged
with light gray fur—
a squirrel is involved.

===

"Alexa, stop," her voice
from next door, the tactile
pleasure of it, of being
familiar with it.

===

Is a professional writer one who
writes for money or
one who professes to?
For what will I exchange this?

===

Could the prayer be made neither
in speech nor writing nor even language
but in some other signifying system?
Hieroglyphs, perhaps? Images, a rebus?
Or in music? Or perhaps
in money? A poem
in money.

===

The dove drops out of its nest
straight to the ground
where it flops, pitifully
with a broken wing.
But when I (9 years old)
get close enough to touch

it miraculously recovers and flies away.

=====

If I point to the mirror on the wall
and say, "me," I speak truly.
And if I break out the mirror
and repeat the gesture to the empty frame,
I again speak truly.
Where it was I must come to be.

=====

Two electricians driving to a job
in the company van, listening to the radio.
All day they string wire through the bones
of a building while the current
of the culture courses through them.

=====

A poet tells me:
"When I'm writing, I try not to read anyone else,
so as not to corrupt my point of view."
A novelist tells me:
"If I read for three hours, I feel guilty because
I think that's time I should have spent writing."
The MFA fantasy is the same
as the capitalist fantasy.

=

Idea for a drawing:
Skeleton with pot belly.

=

When the paths between
meanings meet
in the hollow.

=

Poetry that ancient broken
pottery of sound.

=

The proper name alone
is enough to graft the child
onto the tree of language.
After that, all the
limbs of grammar follow.

=

Why are you in prison?
Because I committed a crime.
What crime did you commit?
The crime of performing an imprisonable act.

═

If you want to
speak truth
say you lie.

═

Discourse reverts
to incantation, last prayer
as the tiger bears down.

═

Duped by
duplicitous nature.

═

The fact that we can
ask the meaning of meaning
means there is none.

═

Tiny signs, least
movement of eye or lip,
smallest inflection of the shoulder,
signs as minuscule as letters
on a page.

Shell, you're feeling
cramped, let's let
some other
hermit camp here.

Appendix: La Police[4]

Can we imagine a world without Police?
The degree to which we consider Police indispensable is the degree
to which Police can be said to be effective.

*

Police crosses all ideological, economic, and political boundaries.
It is an essential feature of contemporary capitalist, communist
and socialist states, of democracies, republics, dictatorships and
monarchies. If a North Korean dictator sees his effigy being
slandered and wants the perpetrators executed, he calls the police.
If an American activist wants to report a landlord showing racial
preference in rental practice, she calls the police. Whether one
wishes to assert his civil rights or to suppress someone else's, one
asserts or suppresses via Police. The very notion of "right," in
both the term's ethical and political dimensions, now denotes a
relationship to Police.
If, as some argue, the human animal has a natural propensity for
language, it would seem it also has a natural propensity for Police.

*

The earliest written record of the term πτόλις (*polis*) is in Hesiod, c.
750 BCE. For the Greeks it referred to the city-state, or sometimes
more specifically to the city's core, the citadel, around which

---

4   *La Police* was written in response to the call by William Allegrezza,
     publisher of Locofo Chaps, shortly after Trump's election, for
     chapbook submissions to send to the White House on the 100th day
     of our 45th president's term. This version is somewhat revised from
     the chapbook. A truncated version was published, also, at LitHub,
     May 3, 2017.

the city developed. The Romans latinized the cognate πολιτεία (*politeia*), "citizenship, administration, civil polity" into *politia*, which was adopted into Middle French as *police*, which in the early 15th century came into English as a direct borrowing, *la police*, a fashionable, gourmet version of "policy" or "public order."

*

The word did not take on its current meaning as a collective noun until 1797 when a group of London merchants pooled funds to hire a band of hooligans to prevent theft of their inventory from the docks, mostly by their own employees. They armed the group with clubs and called them The Police. This metonymy would have sounded a lot like "The Policy" would sound to us now, perhaps even with the same tinge of dark humor. This initial band of 50 men saved the merchants hundreds of thousands in theft prevention, and in 1800 the City of London transformed them from a private to a public organization. The Thames River Police is now the oldest public police organization in the world.

*

Benefits of the new policy spread rapidly along the trade routes of the British empire. Police traveled everywhere the English language did, and soon became the lingua franca of the docks in New York, Dublin, Sydney, Glasgow, etc. Despite a few incidences of trepidation and even revolt, Police came to be the gold standard of governance, world-wide, in only about 50 years. The spread mirrored the rise of English as the language of international trade.

*

Between the *jus imperium* of ancient Rome and the Thames River Police there were knights and church orders, volunteer constables and mercenary bounty hunters, hastily organized posses and stately royal guards, vigilante groups and elected citizenry. There were railroad guards, bridge tenders, tax collectors, ship captains, landlords, field bosses, priests, chiefs, fire brigades and, when things really got out of hand, the cavalry.

Where there had been hundreds of methods there was suddenly only one, and all the others became instantly antique. Henceforth, constables would monitor street lamps. Posses and bounty hunters became nostalgic figures of romance. Royal guards became skeuomorphs, architectural decoration. Vigilante and citizen groups began to be considered as rebels themselves, and the host of lower-level monitors and bosses became bureaucrats and record-keepers.

*

The adoption of French words into English to suggest refinement or class distinction probably dates to the Norman Conquest, that brief period, 1066-1150, when French was the language of the English court. This era of clear linguistic distinction between conquerors and conquered, between the ruling and indentured classes, is apparent in English today in pairings like cook/chef or fashion/couture. Just as, today, restaurants up their star ratings by giving their cooks clean uniforms, *toques blanches* and a French job description, so, in 1800, London stripped the dock roughnecks of their overalls and gave them elegant blue uniforms with matching spiked helmets. Tree limbs and broken oar handles were replaced with fine hardwood clubs produced on lathes to a standard size and polished to a high and uniform gloss. Beards were trimmed and faces washed. The men were arranged in rows, tallest in back, and their elegance recorded for posterity in the brand new medium of photography.

*

The Boys were dressed in Blue explicitly to distinguish them from the red-coated British army, to signal that they were not here to protect, defend and expand borders, but solely to fight the enemy within.

*

Police comes into being to answer a single question: who owns what. The docks are an unruly place where goods belonging to people and entities increasingly removed from the actual location of these goods are being transferred to other owners equally distant. Goods belonging to one factory or farm are commingled with goods from others that are destined for the same port, and this commingling and reordering is done by impoverished dock workers whose interest in the goods they handle is not always abstract. A tear in a bag of flour can become a family's bread that night. A bit off the end of a bolt of cloth might yield a child something to wear to her job at the factory the next day.
The question of who is stealing what from whom can sometimes be answered by visual clues, as when one actually witnesses a worker pocketing a bit of grain or opening a box he is supposed to be merely transporting. But the workers are clever. Sometimes they transfer the goods with stealth rather than clumsy force. A frugal worker might actually accumulate enough wealth to acquire by legal means a watch or a new pair of breeches. So increasingly

Police must rely on less concrete evidence of ownership. They must be literate and mathematically proficient, to be able to check inventories and read bills of lading. They must be able, at least to a limited degree, to write similar documents themselves. The night officer must make a record of the evening's movements of people and goods to hand to the day officer in the morning, and these records must be formalized and consistent, so that if one officer misses a shift due to illness or drunkenness or some other necessity, another can assume that position with no loss of continuity.

Likewise, the Police must know who they are policing. They must know the workers from the bosses and the bosses from the owners. They must know who is actually a worker and who is a thief merely posing as a worker. Hundreds of people come and go on the busy docks; no officer can determine their roles from memory or appearance alone. The way to solve this problem is to assume illegitimacy, to pass this aspect of policing on to the workers themselves. Each worker must prove that he is indeed a worker. A boss must vouch for him, and since the bosses cannot be everywhere at once, each worker must carry a token or sign of the boss's approval.

Police created the modern concept of Identity through this assumption of universal guilt among the working class. One is a thief unless one can prove otherwise. Thievery is not merely punished; it is prevented by this pragmatic measure. Have your identity card or go to gaol.

*

Simultaneously with Police is born the notion of Crime. Like the obverse face of the same coin, negative linguistic pole required to reify the original term, Crime rises into Western consciousness as an urgent necessity, the *raison d'être* of Police.

Crime is the reason for Police, but Police is also the reason for Crime. Just as Police introduces into the diverse and disorderly practices of the protection of the gentry's property a single unified force of suppression, so Crime comes to organize and define the various unseemly activities of the working class rabble. Each is the *not* of the Other, and together they create a social and political knot, a "bootstrap" structure of continually escalating friction, a tangle that widens and gradually ensnares the entire culture.

The tautology itself is perhaps not remarkable, as it merely exemplifies the normal linguistic function of definition by opposition that Saussure and every linguist who came after him observed. But this particular tautology rises with stunning historical rapidity to the status of a central if not universal structure. The moment Police and its obverse are created, they have always existed. Every trace of the historical time before is erased.

*

Crime: mid-13c., "sinfulness," from Old French *crimne* (12c., Modern French *crime*), from Latin *crimen* (genitive *criminis*) "charge, indictment, accusation; crime, fault, offense," perhaps from *cernere* "to decide, to sift" (see *crisis*). But Klein (citing Brugmann) rejects this and suggests *cri-men*, which originally would have been "cry of distress" (Tucker also suggests a root in "cry" words and refers to English *plaint, plaintiff,* etc.). Meaning "offense punishable by law" is from late 14c. The Latin word is glossed in Old English by *facen*, also "deceit, fraud, treachery." *Crime wave* first attested 1893, American English.

*

The TV cop is tired, haggard, an emotional and physical wreck. His or her spouse or partner or child has left or been killed by a criminal or abducted or abused or is in imminent danger of being so. The TV cop is in London or New York or Paris or Toronto or Sydney or Amsterdam. The skyscrapers or slums or brownstones or docks of the City are the backdrop of his or her anguished search for the source of the Crime. His or her desk is awash in file folders or, later, secret databases on a computer screen.

S/he has a drug or alcohol problem, is a recovering addict, sees visions or ghosts, hears haunting echoes of the Crime in memory or in hallucination, carries problematic personal interests into the investigation, is in constant danger of suspension or death or extortion or some other compromise, must constantly vie with unethical forces within the Police or the Polis as well as the citizenry. S/he walks through rooms of the police station or the house or apartment, laden with secret desires and anxieties, but then his or her gaze is suddenly drawn to a photograph on the wall. The photo is on the corkboard in the station or on the wall of a suspect's house or, in the event that s/he has been suspended or fired or is otherwise alienated from the normal comradery of the force, on the wall or coffee table of his or her own apartment or house or condo. The photo reveals to the experienced officer something not at first apparent to the viewer or to the other characters in the drama, some small hint, a facial expression or previously unnoticed contiguity of space and time, revealing an alibi to be questionable or an outright lie, turning a friendly witness into a suspect or vice versa. S/he stares at the photo, suddenly entranced, leaning in to study it in minute detail. The depth of field shortens, and the image of the office or apartment in the background blurs. The sounds of the culture begin to fade and an ominous music rises. S/

he takes out the tack and looks at it even more closely.

*

Photography has held, from its beginnings in the early 19th century, a special place in the arsenal of Police weaponry. As a kind of public relations tool, the Police and the military were among the first to use it to put forth their public face, archival representation of order and symmetry. Carefully posed, uniforms immaculate, not a hair out of place, arrayed in order of rank and seniority, the Police placed itself at the beginning of history by placing itself at the beginning of the new technology that will, henceforth, record it.

But public relations was not the only utility Police found in the new medium. Just as Crime is the obverse of the Police itself, the mugshot is the flip side of the PR photo. Unposed and unadorned, fresh from interrogation or clubbing, filth of the street still apparent and without benefit of tonsorial detailing, the Criminal, too, is recorded into the archive. The mugshot is placed in the file, stapled to the record of the life: name or names, place of residence, date and place of birth, employment history, spouse(s), children, parents, siblings, and of course the record of criminal activities and arrests.

The mugshot itself—with its backdrop of chipped plaster and peeling paint, with its messy hair, its small chalkboard with an identification number and a list of crimes—is proof of the subject's criminality. If, in the past, a citizen's infractions against property owners or the state were treated as activities requiring this or that mode of redress, after the institution of the Police, Crime becomes a matter of Identity, a genetic code that belongs to the person as opposed to the act, and remains in the front of the file no matter the further course of the Subject's life. "Crime" is no longer an action but a proclivity, a "personality trait," a disease. The mother doesn't resort to theft or prostitution because her children are starving but because of the Crime she carries within herself, within her body.

Increasingly, the new science of Psychology and the ancient arts of Medicine will be called upon to address Crime. The new surgical technique of lobotomy is created as an attempt to excise Crime from the worker's body surgically. Criminals are sterilized to prevent them from passing Crime on to future generations. The new and epistemologically rigorous "science" of Criminology is created to study and classify the various forms of the disease.

*

Originally invented to address the very specific problem of theft by workers, Police quickly expands its domain along this axis of Identity. The police file grows to contain more and more information. It can include, along with actual criminal acts, all sorts of anecdotal "evidence": work records, testimony, denunciations by neighbors, rumors of bad behavior, sexual transgressions, etc. And these elements of criminal identity quickly become associated, themselves, with the realm of Crime. Thus the role of the Police comes to include the monitoring of almost every realm of activity of its Subjects, everything from sexual practice to the payment of taxes.

It even becomes possible to envision crimes which consist in nothing more than the manipulation of Identity itself: stealing or forging files, giving false information to trick the Police, etc. Crime attains an intellectual mystique, and the Police, far from the ax-handle-wielding brute on the dock, becomes in popular conception the professorial Detective, a master of deduction, genius in the study of texts, images and logic. The Detective can hear the lie in a

Subject's tone of voice, can ferret out a contradiction between two files or statements, or pick the Criminal out of room full of innocent civilians by means of the subtlest clues.

Thus the Police steps off the docks and onto the stage of 19th-century media. Like the knights of yore, Police became the privileged protagonist of literature. As knights were to the Romance, Police became the indomitable hero-class of the novel, the *nouveau roman*. If the virtuous, chivalric knight captured the imaginations and carried the functional ideologies of medieval Europe, the depiction of the Police that will do this for the reading public of the 19th century is that of the brilliant detective.

*

While the form is sometimes said to have originated in the impossibly brilliant deductions of Voltaire's *Zadig* (1748), the detective story is launched to the realm of a genre by the publication of Poe's "The Murders in the Rue Morgue" a century later. As in the host of imitators that would follow on Poe's lead, the Detective here is not, himself, a Policeman. Dupin is an enigmatic character, aloof, anti-social, literate as a professor of philosophy and beyond that possessed of superhuman powers of logic and deduction. The Policemen in the story, like their progenitors on the London Docks, are simian brutes by comparison. They come to Dupin because the crime is an intellectual labyrinth beyond their powers to map. Dupin leads them, by means of careful analysis of texts and speech, through a maze of identities to the one point they had never considered, that the perpetrator might have no Identity. That is, that it might not be human.

*

To be human is to have an Identity on file with the Police. I have a mugshot, therefore I am.

*

But the meta-work of the 19th century is Poe's third story featuring the intrepid Dupin, "The Purloined Letter." Like *Hamlet*, "The Purloined Letter" is a tale of a compromised queen and cuckolded king, and the differences between these two iconic works reveal historical changes that have occurred in the interim, changes in the roles of monarchs and citizens.

In "The Purloined Letter" Hamlet's part is taken by the Police. In place of Hamlet's anguished, dream-haunted search for the truth of his father's murder and his mother's seduction, Poe posits a meticulous search by the Police, not for the truth of the Crime and its instigator, but rather for the text that bears that truth. Neither we, Dupin, nor the Police will know the content of that text, the eponymous letter; we do not know what it says, only that what it says is the truth, and that it is a truth which is not for us to know. The role of the Police is, in fact, to keep this truth secret.

Left to deduce the content of the letter from our own fecund imaginations, we conclude it represents the Queen's infidelity, though it could just as well be, say, evidence of embezzlement, a land-swap for influence, or an agreement trading a nephew's corporate appointment for a building permit.

Hamlet's investigation is to uncover the facts of the Crime, to know who did what, and how and when. For the Police of "The Purloined Letter" the goal is exactly the opposite. It is to not-know the truth; to know that the truth exists and control its circulation, yet without knowing what that truth is. To find the letter and hand it, still sealed, back to the Queen.[5]

Hamlet is a tragedy, representing, with other of Shakespeare's plays, a modernization of the ancient genre, and it's characters are, in respect to both the genre and the events that unfold within it, slaves to history, which is represented as an implacable moral force guiding them irresistably toward the revelation of the truth. "The Purloined Letter," by contrast, is a comedy in which the players are saved from both history and the truth by an amoral force of suppression which works with meticulous efficiency to conceal the royal sin. The play within the play in *Hamlet* reveals Gertrude's and Claudius's crime, but at the center of Poe's story is a drawn curtain which the brilliant Dupin and the inept Police (the first iteration, no doubt, of the Keystone Cops) faithfully guard, adjusting the folds to maintain the Queen Mother's privacy with never a peek inside.

Inside the "locked box" of the Queen's boudoir there is another, smaller, locked box, which is the text that describes the box, this text. Inside the cordon *La police* makes around the Queen, there is a second cordon, this one around the letter, the truth itself. The uniformed bodies of Police stand in front of it, facing out.

*

The Police system, originally formulated as a protection for factory owners and merchants, spread with the Industrial Revolution. As the bosses' muscle, it became an essential part of the mass production scenario and an emblem of British efficiency and colonial domination. Patrick Colquhoun, who founded the Thames River Police, used arguments from Jeremy Bentham to

---

5   It might be said that Rosencrantz and Guildenstern, Hamlet's hapless dupes who carry their own execution order to the monarch, foreshadow the role of Police in the detective novel.

convince the merchants' association to give the new system a try, and Bentham's utopian vision of a working class under total and constant surveillance underlies the workings of Police to this day. But because of their ground-breaking work in Identity creation, the role of the Police—and the realm of Crime—quickly expands beyond the docks and factories into every facet of human life. Everything that might be logged on a worker's Identity Card— employment and marital status, sexual practice, alcohol and drug use, skin tone, race, ethnicity, religion, nationality, place and time of birth, family organization—becomes relevant to the subject's relationship to Crime and the Police.

In the end, everyone will have a mugshot. Everyone will have a file, a number, an Identity. Everyone will be, to one degree or another, a criminal. Identity structures the whole Earth as a prison.

*

While the implications of the mass production of images have been explored by Walter Benjamin and his many disciples, photography as a constitutive factor in the development of Police practice and the establishment of Identity as an objective and internalized mode of state control has not, to date, been appreciated for its importance in the evolution of the species. The light image is not simply a new character set in humanity's font library; it is a whole new mode of signification which will affect and in important ways supplant all the others. Muybridge's sequential images of Leland Stanford's galloping racehorse didn't simply explain to us how a horse runs; they *proved* it beyond any argument that the suddenly antique arts of painting, anatomy, philosophy, aesthetics, or mathematics, could ever present. Photography, whether it documents a crime scene or a cat playing with string, is *evidence*, obtaining to a prosecutorial function that painting or any other signifying art can never aspire to. The photograph became the reality that handcrafted arts are measured against.

And this effect was not limited to the arts. Freud's discovery of the unconscious and the significance of dreams can be read as another product of the new photographic imagination. Freud saw the dream as a series of two-dimensional images possessing the evidentiary qualities of forensic photos, revealing a past lost to the imperfections of memory and a subject the subject itself would not recognize.

Once the photograph was loosed in the world, we might say, the world became a photograph, and Freud leaned close with his loupe. To imagine that this historic upheaval in the nature of the image and Freud's concern with it were unrelated, to think that this convergence between the history of technology and the history of ideas was a matter of simple chance, would be naive.

*

The mugshot begat the passport photo begat the selfie. And now this badge we carry on our lapels from cradle to grave is the source of all embarrassment and arrogance, every disgrace and every honor. We long to add to our file our accomplishments, our books and degrees and years of service to employers, and we pray to have our sins, our petty thefts and sexual wanderings, erased. We view with envy the Identity Cards of our superiors and with derision or condescending pity those of our underlings.

But the one thought that never occurs to anyone, the notion that remains as unthinkable as a world without Police, is that we might live naked, unclassified, unphotographed, and unlabelled. The thought is horrible, source of existential despair, the sickness unto death. Without Identity we drift like ephemeral butterflies, briefly alive and disappearing without a trace.

About the Author

Bill Lavender is a poet, novelist, musician, carpenter and publisher living in New Orleans. For 15 years he worked at the University of New Orleans, as director of the Low Residency MFA program and later as Editor-in-Chief of UNO Press. He founded his own press, Lavender Ink, in 1995, and added the Diálogos imprint, devoted to cross-cultural literatures (mostly in translation), in 2011. He is the co-founder, with Megan Burns of Trembling Pillow Press, of the New Orleans Poetry Festival.